PENTATONIC MASTER

97 Warm-ups to
Revolutionize Your
Guitar Playing

The Missing Method
An imprint of
Tenterhook Books, LLC
Akron, Ohio

Christian J. Triola

Copyright ©2018, 2020 Christian J. Triola, Amy Joy Triola

All Rights Reserved.

Except as permitted under the U.S. Copyright Act of 1976, no part of this publication may be reproduced, distributed, or transmitted, in whole or in part, in any form or by any means, or stored in any form of retrieval system, without prior written consent of the author.

Bulk sales inquiries can be directed to the author at info@themissingmethod.com.

Cover and Book Design by Amy Joy, ©2018 Amy Joy

The Missing Method™ for Guitar is an imprint of Tenterhook Books, LLC. The Missing Method name and logos are property of Tenterhook Books, LLC.
First Edition 2018, Tenterhook Books, LLC. Akron, Ohio.

Library of Congress Control Number: 2020911782

ISBN-13: 978-1953101075 (Paperback)

Table of Contents

About the Author i
   What is the Missing Method? i

Introduction 1
   How this Book Works 1
   Overview & Recommended Approach 2

Basic Techniques 3
   Fret Hand Technique 4
   How to Play Warm-Up #1 6

Unit 1: Open Position 6
   How to Play Warm-Up #2 8
   How to Play Warm-Up #3 9
   Position 1 (Open Position) E Minor Pentatonic Pattern . . . 10
   How to Play Warm-Up #4 11
   How to Play Warm-Up #5 12
   How to Play Warm-Up #6 13
   How to Play Warm-Up #7 15
   How to Play Warm-Up #8 16
   How to Play Warm-Up #12 19

Unit 2: Position 2 G Major Pentatonic Scale 20
   Position 2 G Major Pentatonic Pattern 21
   How to Play Warm-Up #15 21

Unit 3: Position 3 32
   Position 3 G Major/E Minor Pentatonic Pattern 34

Unit 4: Position 4 43
   Position 4 G Major/E Minor Pentatonic Pattern 45

Unit 5: Position 5 54
Position 5 G Major/E Minor Pentatonic Pattern. 55

Unit 6: Position 6 64
Position 6 G Major/E Minor Pentatonic Pattern. 65

Appendix 77
How to Tune Your Guitar. 78
Guitar Tuners and Other Tuning Resources 80
How to Read Tablature 81

The Elements of Reading Music 82
The Staff 82
Ledger Lines 83
Understanding Time 83
Eighth Notes 85
Sixteenth Notes. 85
Keeping Time: How to Use Your Metronome 86
The 5 Positions of the Pentatonic Scale. 89

Resources to Help You Take Your Playing Further . . 90

About the Author 91
What is the Missing Method? 91

Introduction

Five notes, endless possibilities. That's the best way to describe the pentatonic scale. It is a five note scale ("penta" meaning five; "tonic" referring to tones) used in every style of western music to some degree, from classical and jazz to punk and classic rock. For the guitar player, it is the essential scale. It sounds good; it fits over the fretboard perfectly; and it can be used to help any new player invent a solo relatively quickly.

Now that you've either worked your way through Technique Master Volume 1 or have already in some way developed strong basic technique, you are ready to take your skills to a higher level. That's where scales come into play. A scale is essentially a collection of pitches that sound good together within a musical context. By learning to play scales, not only do you become familiar with all the possible notes in a key, but you also train your ear to recognize the sound of the scale. Therefore, the warm-ups that are presented in this book are designed to improve three areas of your playing: fretboard and scale knowledge; your ear; and your technique, including finger strength, accuracy, and dexterity.

How this Book Works

This book is designed to help you continue building your technique while mastering the pentatonic scale. Each section takes you through a different region of the neck, so you can learn the scale from the open strings all the way up to the fifteenth fret. While you are doing that, you will be asked to focus on your technique and timing, so don't neglect those important details. Each unit starts off with a simple version of either the major or minor pentatonic scale. Then you work on all the possible notes of the scale in that position. Next, the scale is mixed up in a variety of ways to help you further cement your knowledge of the scale. Finally, each section ends with a review, as well as example licks to give you ideas of how you might use the scale to create your own musical lines.

All the scales and licks presented in this book are shown in both standard notation as well as tablature.

Overview & Recommended Approach

Be sure to practice every single warm-up and lick in this book with a metronome. If you've successfully completed Technique Master Volume 1, then I'm sure you are already very familiar with how to use a metronome. However, if you don't have much metronome experience, a section on how to use a metronome is include in every one of the books in the Technique Master Series, including this one. You'll find it in the appendix. Like everything having to do with music, it takes time and practice to get comfortable using a metronome, but it is well worth the momentary discomfort. Basically: don't give up on the metronome!

Next, I'd also recommend humming or singing each exercise in this book as you learn them. That way, you will be able to connect your ear to what your fingers are doing. You are essentially internalizing the sound, which will help you develop your overall musicianship. You don't have to be a good singer; you just have to vocalize the pitches to help you better understand them.

It should be noted that this book thoroughly explores the pentatonic scale in the key of E minor and its relative major, G major. After you learn this key, it is highly recommended that you move the scale patterns around the neck to learn them in other keys as well.

Final note: don't neglect your tuning. Always check your tuning before playing your guitar. This may seem like an obvious thing to mention, but not all guitar players pay attention to this vital detail.

So good luck, pay close attention to detail, and don't forget to use your metronome!

Basic Techniques

How to hold the pick

1. First, curve the fingers of your picking hand inward, while keeping them relaxed. Don't make a fist.

2. Second, place the pick on top of the first knuckle, so that the point of the pick faces outward.

3. Third, place your thumb over the pick to hold it in place. This may feel awkward or uncomfortable at first, but once you get used to it, you'll have full control over the pick.

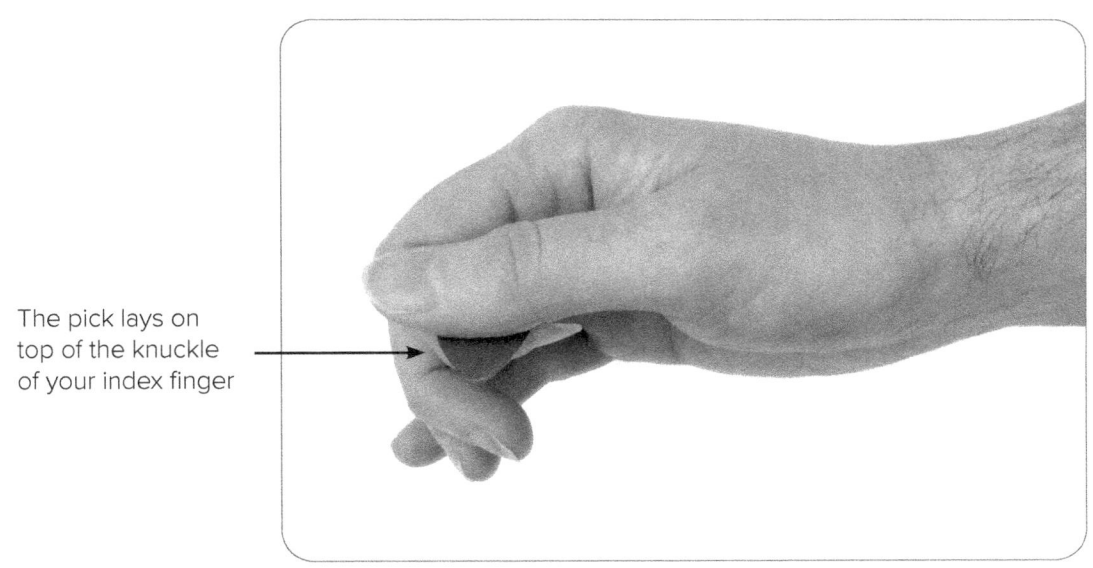

The pick lays on top of the knuckle of your index finger

Fret Hand Technique

Proper fret hand technique is crucial to getting a good sound and avoiding injury.

1. First, always keep your fingers up on their tips. The fingers should be spread apart and not touching each other.

2. Second, the wrist should be dropped down and the thumb planted behind the neck so that the thumb falls between the first and second fingers when looking at it from above.

3. Third, the knuckles of your hand should be running completely parallel to the neck, and the palm of your hand should not make contact with the neck.

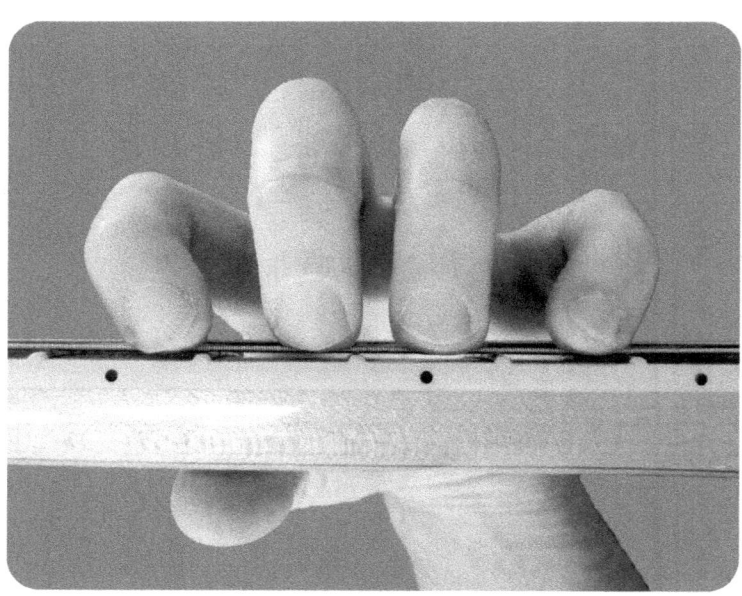

Units 1-5

The Five Positions of the Pentatonic Scale

Unit 1: Open Position

How to Play Warm-Up #1

Warm-up #1 gives you the E minor pentatonic scale in one octave, first ascending, then descending. It is designed to help you start learning the pentatonic scale while you warm-up, as well as get the basic sound of the scale in your ear. As we progress through this book, this scale will be one of two primary sounds from which all other warm-ups are based.

When playing scales on the guitar, oftentimes you are given all the possible notes in one region or position of the neck. If you were playing piano, or many other instruments, you usually learn a scale from its root and play all the notes in order until you reach the octave. That's why we are starting off with a one octave scale rather than a typical guitar-style box pattern.

1. To begin, play through the warm-up to try it out. Make sure each note is clear as you play. Don't try to play it fast yet.

2. Next, you'll want to work out your fingering:
   - Play the 4th string, second fret with the second finger.
   - Play the 3rd string, second fret with the second finger.
   - Play the 2nd string, third fret with the third finger.
   - All other notes are played open, of course.

3. Next, set your *metronome to about 60 beats per minute (bpm). Then tap your foot *with* the click before you play anything. Once you are in sync with the click, begin playing the warm-up. Make sure each note is played with the click, not after it. Once you've played the exercise a

few times perfectly with the metronome, increase the speed by either five or ten clicks (65 to 70bpm). Tap your foot again, and then play the exercise several more times until you can play it perfectly at the new speed. Continue doing this until you reach about 120 to 130 bpm. You can push yourself faster than that if you so desire.

A final note: Even though warm-up 1 is fairly easy to play, do not neglect your technique. Make sure your wrist is dropped, your hands are comfortable, and your knuckles are parallel to the neck and not at any kind of angle. Refer to the picture on page 4 to see what your hand should look like. And always keep your fingers up on their tips.

If you have not practiced with a metronome before, see the section in the Appendix called: How to Use a Metronome.

Warm-Up #1

How to Play Warm-Up #2

Warm-up #2 contains the same notes as warm-up #1 but is an octave lower.

To begin, as before, simply try it out. It's an easy one to play, so it shouldn't take long to figure out.

Then work out your fingering:

- Play the 6th string, third fret with the third finger.
- Play the 5th string, second fret with the second finger.
- Play the 4th string, second fret with the second finger.

Avoid hopping around using only one finger. Though it is possible to do so with this exercise, it is not recommended, as it creates poor technique habits.

Again, set your metronome to a comfortable, yet slow beat, around 60 bpm. Always tap your foot to sync up with the metronome before playing. Once you feel that you have the beat, begin playing along with the click as before. Play the exercise several times perfectly before moving on to a faster beat.

Once you can easily play it correctly, increase the speed by five or ten clicks. Continue like this until 120 to 130 bpm, or until you find yourself unable to keep up with the metronome.

Warm-Up #2

How to Play Warm-Up #3

Warm-up #3 is the classic box pattern of the E minor pentatonic scale. This pattern is the most widely used of the pentatonic scale patterns. It fits easily under your fingers and sounds cool regardless of musical genre.

First, simply try it out. If you've never played this pattern before you'll quickly see that it is a combination of the first two warm-ups in this book. It covers two full octaves plus on extra note beyond the second octave.

Use the following fingering:

- Play the 6th string, third fret with the third finger.
- Play the 5th string, second fret with the second finger.
- Play the 4th string, second fret with the second finger.
- Play the 3rd string, second fret with the second finger.
- Play the 2nd string, third fret with the third finger.
- Play the 1st string, third fret with the third finger.
- All other notes are played open, of course.

Don't forget the metronome

As with the previous exercises, set your metronome to around 60bpm and get in sync with the beat by tapping your foot. Then, as before, play along with the click until you can play the whole pattern easily and perfectly. Once you have it, start increasing the speed as before (in increments of 5 to 10 bpm). For this one, challenge yourself to see how fast you can get it. But work up to it.

Position 1 (Open Position) E Minor Pentatonic Pattern

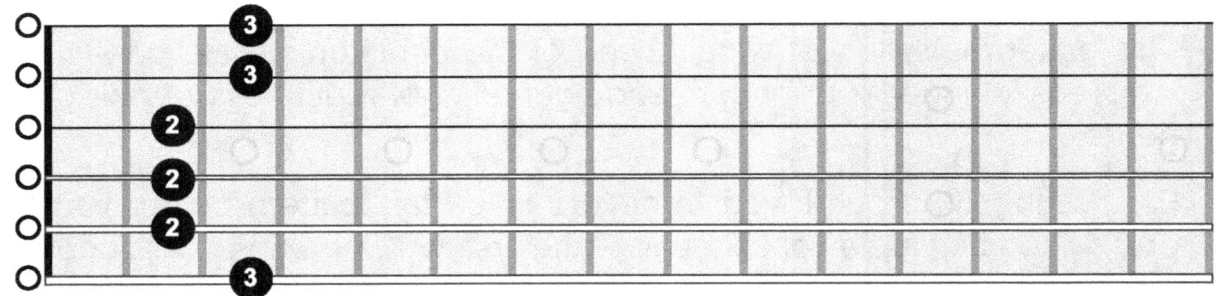

Warm-Up #3

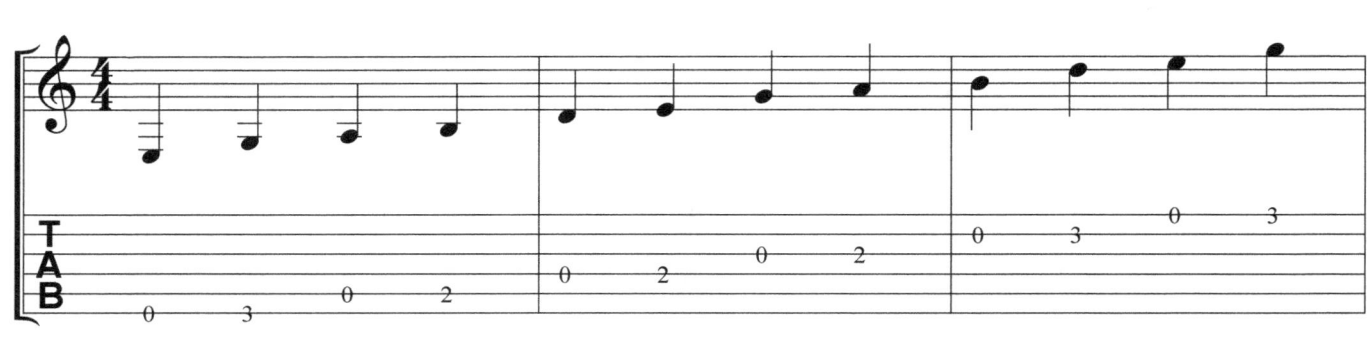

How to Play Warm-Up #4

Warm-up #4 is a variation on warm-up #3. This time, however, the quarter notes have been replaced with eighth notes. This means that you will now need to use alternate picking, shifting some of the focus to your picking hand. (Alternate picking simply means you pick down and up alternately. Here you will pick down on the beat and up on the offbeat).

When playing eighth notes with a metronome, you will now play two even notes per click. A good way to do this is to first tap your foot as usual along with the click. Then think: when your foot goes down, the pick goes down, as your foot comes up, the pick plays up. Be careful not to rush the second half of the beat; make sure it is played exactly between clicks.

⊓ = Strum Down

V = Strum Up

Warm-Up #4

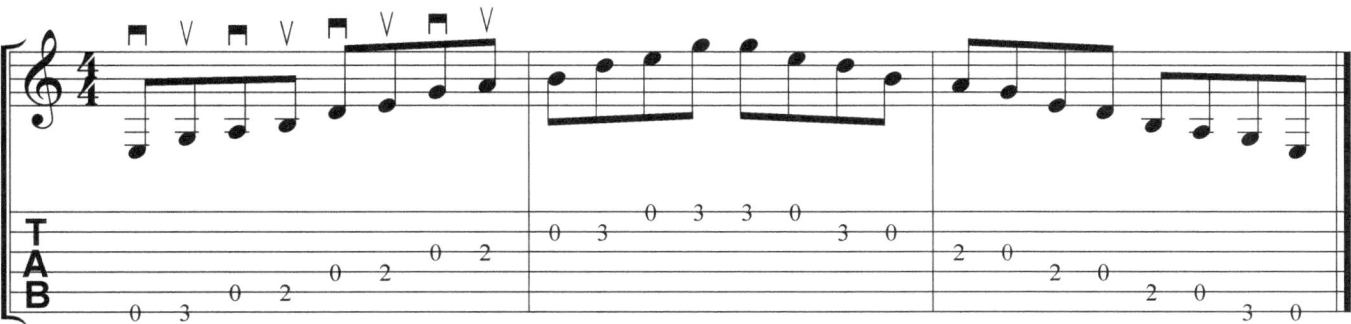

How to Play Warm-Up #5

Warm-up #5 is another variation on warm-up #3. This time the eighth notes have been replaced with sixteenth notes. This means that you will now play four even notes per click of the metronome, so be sure to keep this one slow until you can do this comfortably.

To sync up sixteenth notes to your metronome, start again by tapping your foot with the click. Play one note as your foot taps, followed by a second just before it rises. Then play a third note as your foot is at its highest point, then a fourth just before your foot hits the ground again for the next beat. Be sure to count them like this: ONE-eee-and-uh, TWO-eee-and-uh, THREE-eee-and-uh, FOUR-eee-and-uh. (The numbers are played with the click; the ands are played between the clicks, and the eee and uh are played between the number and the *and* respectively.)

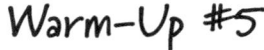

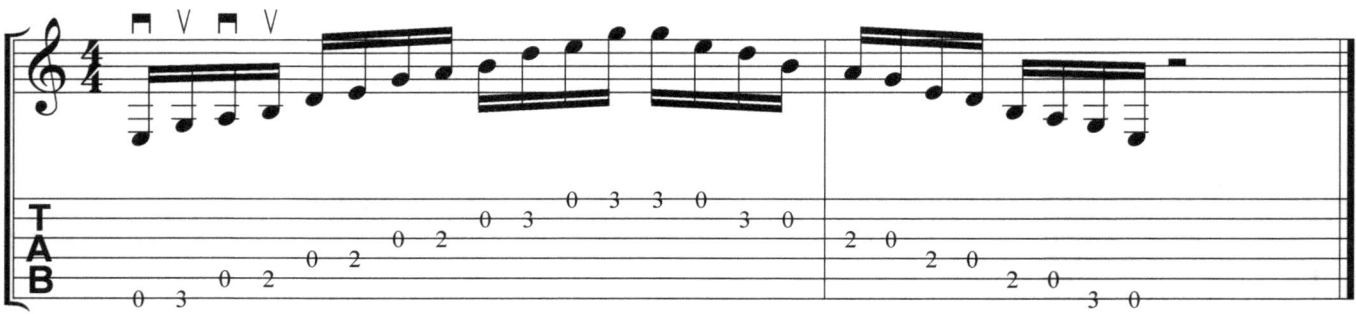

How to Play Warm-Up #6

Warm-up #6 returns to quarter notes and presents a new variation on the pentatonic scale. Instead of playing through the scale note by note, we will now play it by going up three notes and then back one as we progress through the open position box pattern.

Be sure to use your metronome, pick downward only, since we are using quarter notes, and gradually build up speed as you practice this warm-up. Start at about 60 bpm and try to get it to at least 120 bpm before moving on to the next exercise.

Warm up #6 begins on the following page.

Warm-Up #6

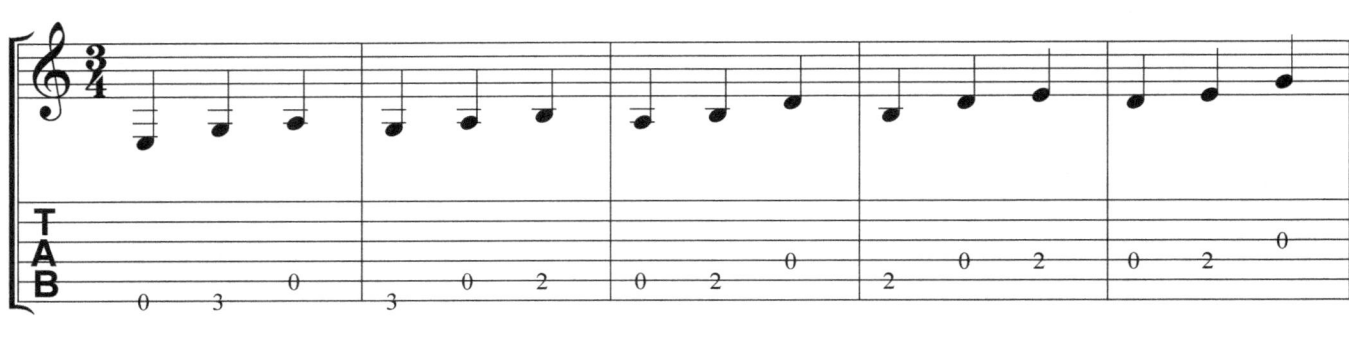
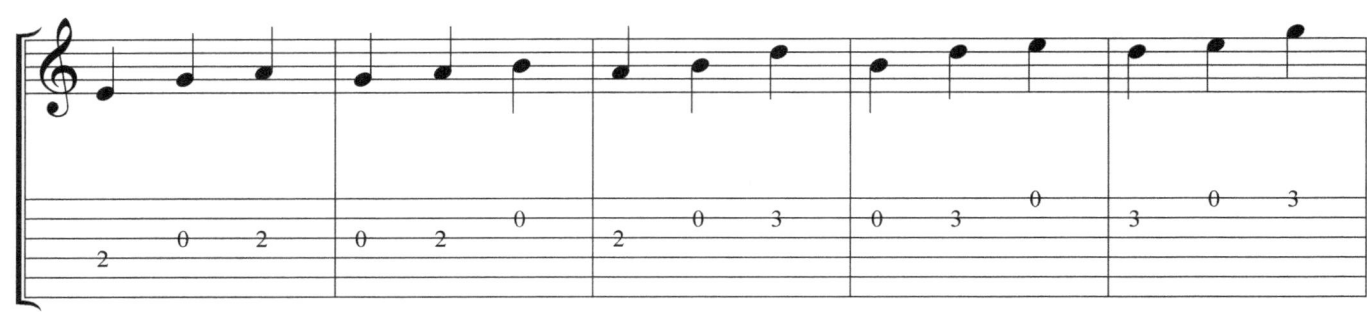
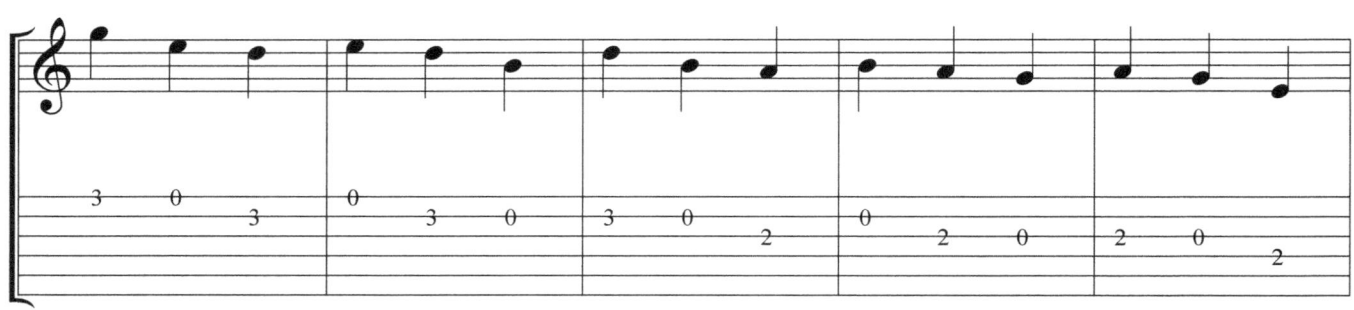
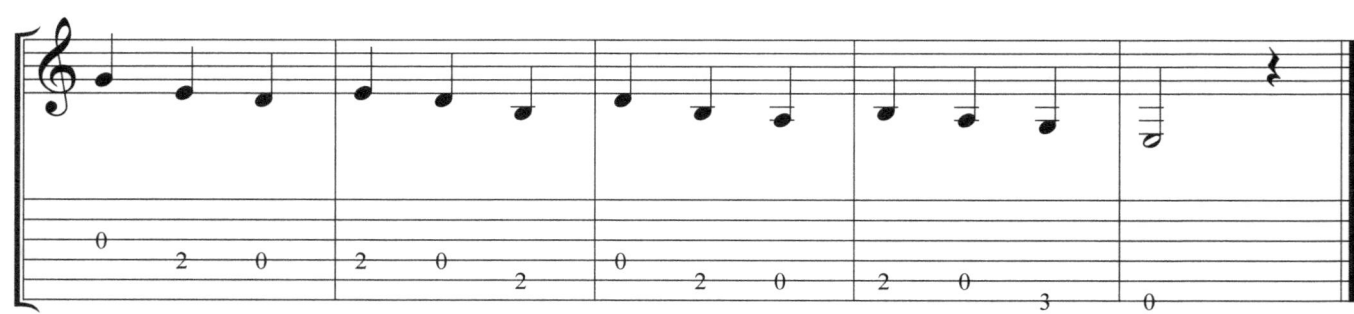

How to Play Warm-Up #7

Warm-up #7 is a variation on warm-up #6, however, instead of regular eighth notes, this exercise uses eighth note triplets.

To play triplets along with your metronome, play three even notes per click. Pick down on the initial beat, up on middle note of the triplet, and then down again for the last portion of the triplet. This forces you to play two quick down-picks when moving from triplet to triplet. Therefore, it is recommended to try out the triplet feel on an open string, practicing with just your picking hand, before attempting the exercise.

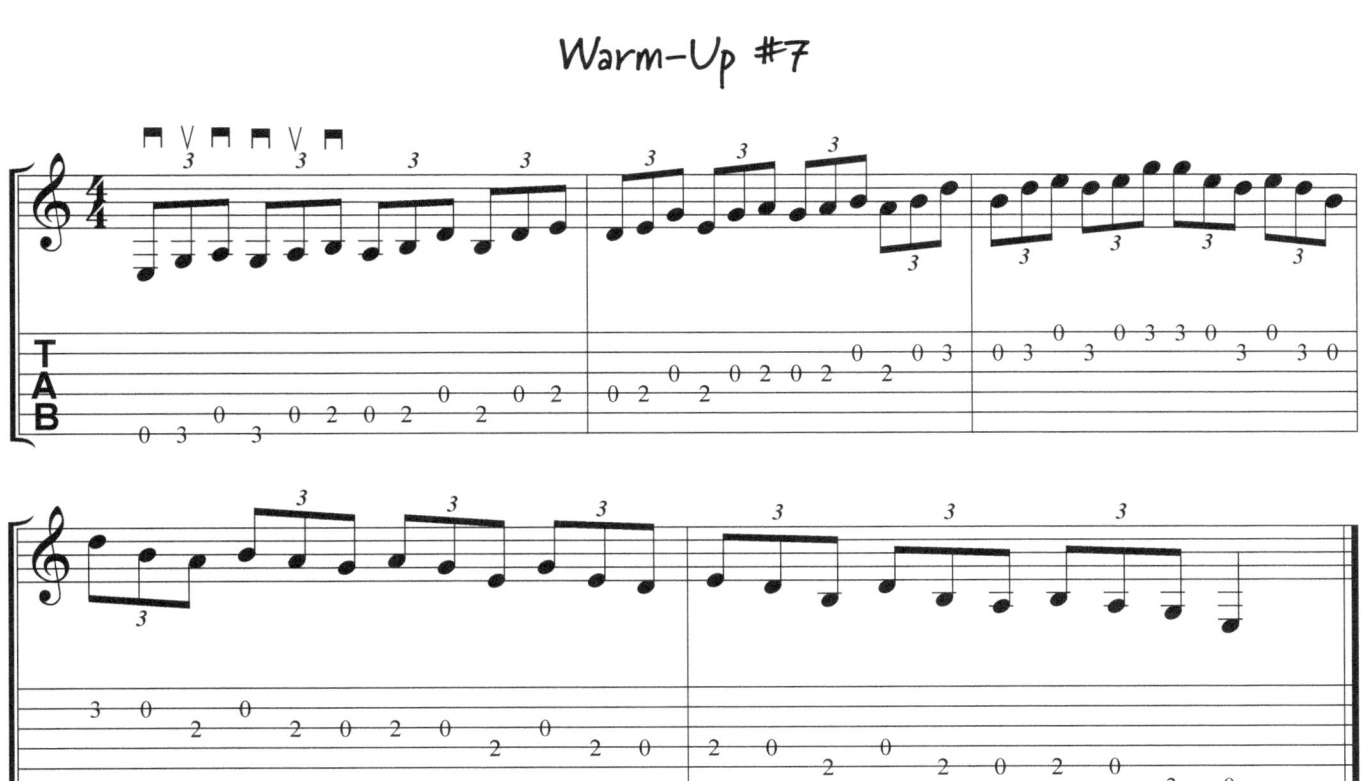

How to Play Warm-Up #8

Warm-up #8 is another variation of warm-up #6, this time with sixteenth notes.

Instructions on how to practice with sixteenth notes can be found along with the instructions to warm-up #5.

Warm-Up #8

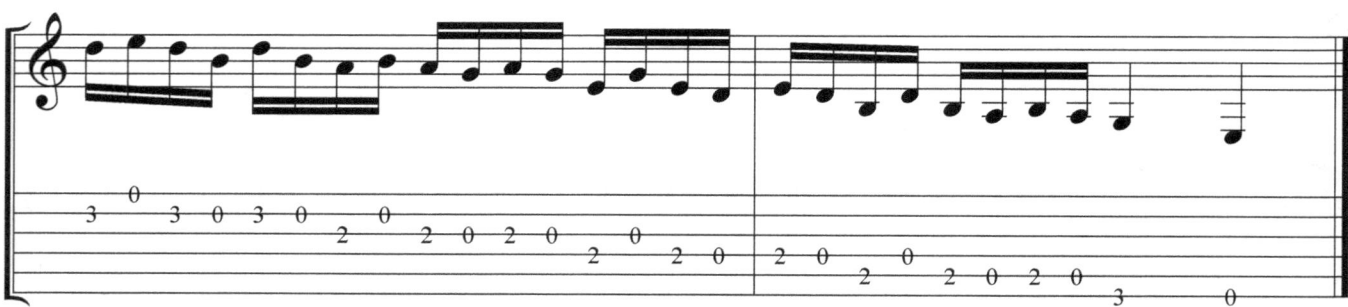

Warm-Up #9

Warm-up #9 takes the E minor pentatonic scale and mixes the notes up further. This time you will play a note of the scale, skip the next note, then come back and play the missed note.

As usual, start off slowly, watch your technique, use correct fingering, and practice it with the metronome.

Warm-Up #10

Warm-up #10 is the eighth note version of warm-up #9. Be sure to alternate your picking.

Warm-Up #11

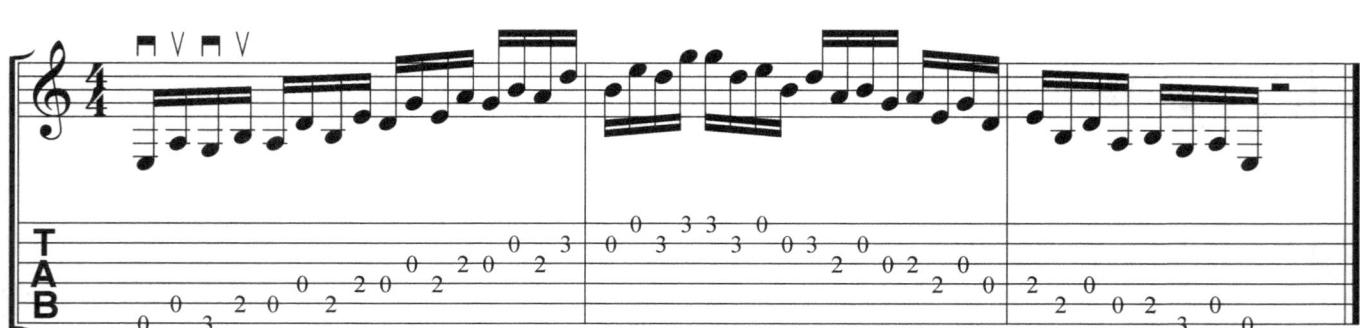

How to Play Warm-Up #12

Warm-up #12 brings us back to the full E minor pentatonic box pattern. However, this time you are being asked to include hammer-ons and pull-offs. When ascending, pick on the first half of every eighth note pair and then hammer-on (without picking again) to the next note. When descending, pick the first note, and then pull-off for the second note.

Warm-Up #12

Unit 2: Position 2 G Major Pentatonic Scale

In Unit 2, we will move up the neck into the next pentatonic pattern. This pattern starts on the note G, rather than E, and is essentially, the G major pentatonic pattern when played from the root. As in the last unit, we will start off by playing the G major pentatonic scale in one octave groups, one high, one low. Then we will explore the full pattern in the same manner as the last unit.

Warm-ups #13 and #14, get you started with the G major pentatonic scale in one octave, using quarter notes.

Warm-Up #13

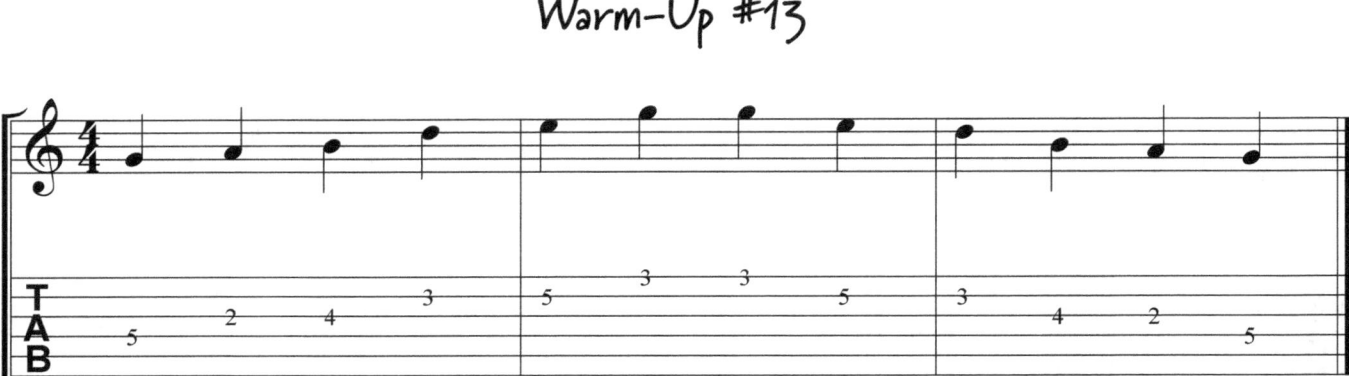

Warm-Up #14

How to Play Warm-Up #15

Warm-up #15 is the full G major pentatonic pattern.

Warm-up #15 (Position 2) fingering

To start:

- Use your second finger for the note G on the 6th string, third fret. Then use your fourth finger (pinky) for the note A on the 6th string, fifth fret.

In general:

- Use your first finger for any note played on the second fret.
- Use your second finger for any note played on the third fret.
- Use your third finger for any note played on the fourth fret.
- Use your fourth finger for any note played on the fifth fret.

Position 2 G Major Pentatonic Pattern

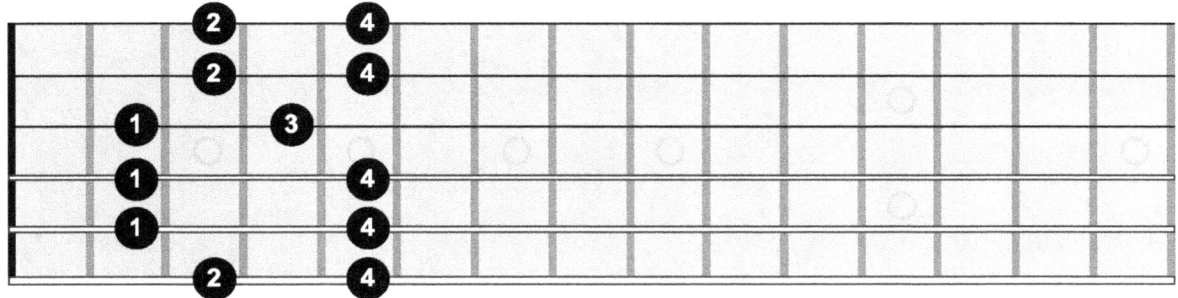

Warm-Up #15

Warm-Up #16

Warm-Up #17

Warm-Ups #18, #19, and #20

The next three warm-ups use the full G major pentatonic pattern, but this time they move up three notes and then fall back one. Reminder: watch your technique, and use correct and consistent fingering throughout each warm-up.

Warm-Up #18

Warm-Up #19

Warm-Up #20

Warm-Ups #21, #22, and #23

The following set of warm-ups have you skipping every other note of the scale as you ascend and then descend. Be sure to watch your fingerings, and as always, build speed and coordination using a metronome in the same manner as in the previous warm-ups.

Warm-Up #21

Warm-Up #22

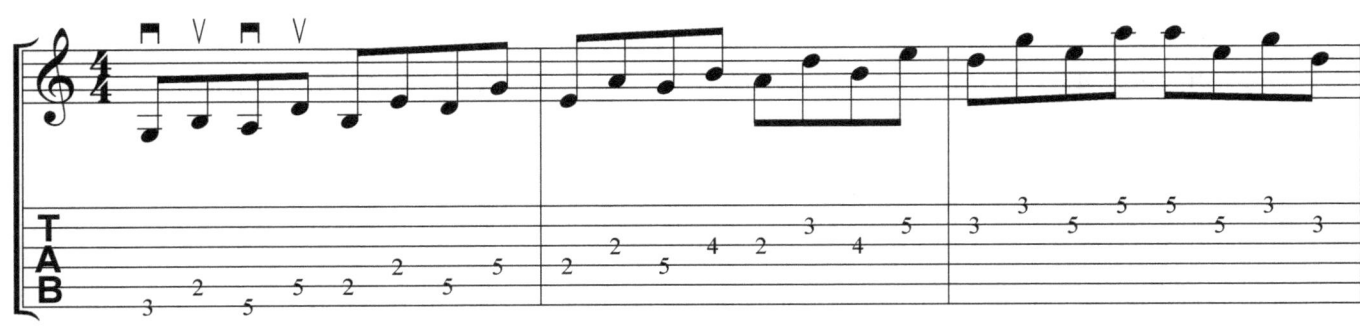

Warm-Up #23

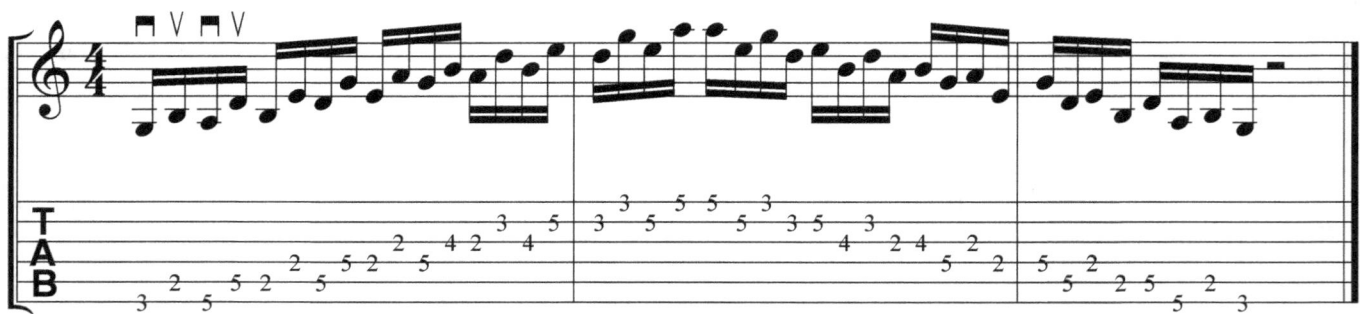

Warm-Up #24

In this warm-up, you'll want to hammer-on when ascending and pull-off when descending.

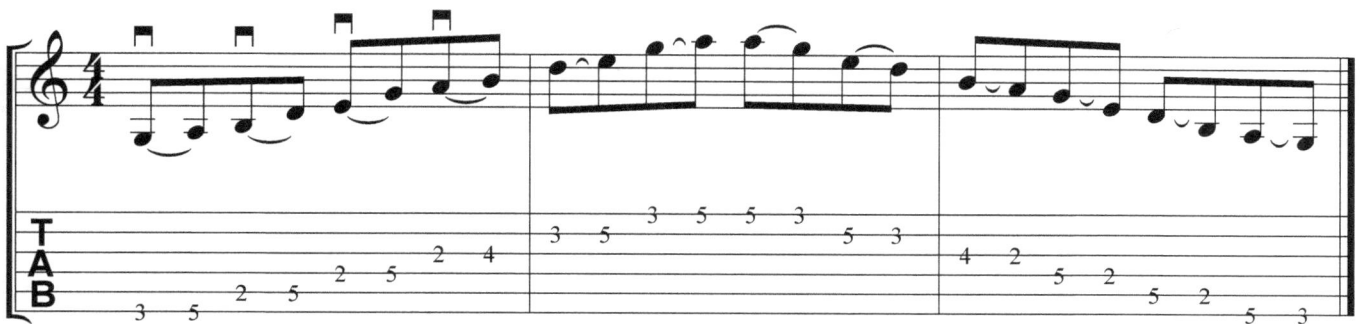

Warm-Ups #25 and #26

Warm-ups #25 and #26 combine notes from position one (see Unit 1) and position 2. Even if you are more comfortable reading the standard notation, be sure to look at the tablature to make sure you are playing it as intended.

Warm-Up #25

Warm-Up #26

Warm-Ups #27, #28, and #29

The following warm-ups are licks to give you ideas on how the scales can be used in a musical setting. Instead of just playing through scale notes, licks are examples of what you can do with the scale notes. They are essentially short melodic phrases, like a sentence, from which you can create your own ideas. The best way to use licks is to learn them in multiple keys, and adapt them to your unique style of playing.

Warm-Up #27
Lick 1

Warm-Up #28
Lick 2

Lick #2 is an alternate version of lick #1. Both use the same notes, but are played differently. Refer to the tablature to see the differences.

Warm-Up #29
Lick 3

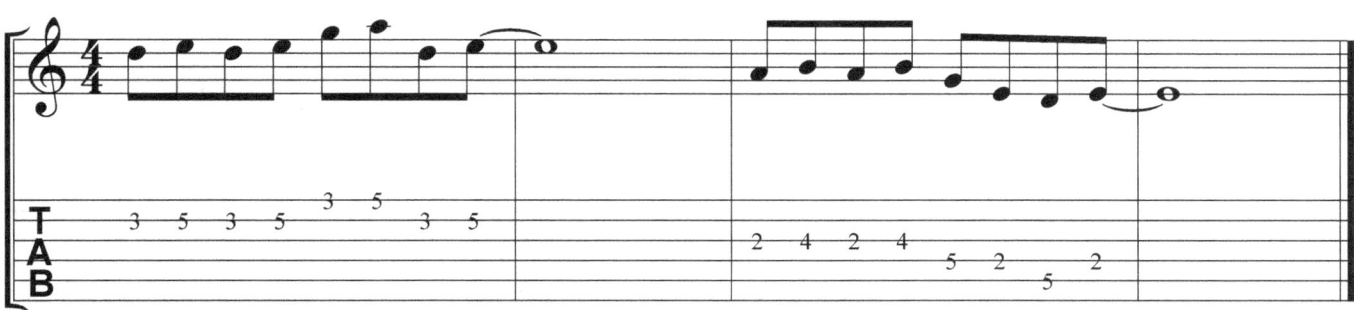

Unit 3: Position 3
G Major/E Minor Pentatonic Scale

The G major scale and E minor pentatonic scale contain the same set of notes. G major starts on G, and E minor starts on E. However, this third position does not start on either one of these notes, so it can be seen as either G major pentatonic starting on the A, or as E minor pentatonic starting on the A. It just depends on which note, the G or the E, is being used as the root of the scale.

Warm-up #30 makes G the root and gives you a chance to play through the G major pentatonic scale in this position. Whereas warm-up #31 takes you through E minor pentatonic.

Warm-Up #30

Warm-Up #31

Warm-Ups #32, #33, and #34

Warm-ups #32, #33, #34 use the full box pattern in this position. Make sure your wrist is dropped, fingers are on their tips, and that you make full use of your metronome. Again, start slowly around 60 bpm and after you master that speed increase the speed in increments of 5 to 10 clicks.

Position 3 Fingering

To start:

- Use your first finger for the note A on the 6th string, fifth fret. Then use your third finger for the note B on the 6th string, seventh fret.

In general:

- Use your first finger for any note played on the 5th fret. However, this position does have one exception to that rule. On the third string, you will want to use your first finger on 4th fret and your fourth finger on the 7th fret.

- Use your third finger for any note played on 7th fret. (Except on the third string).

- Use your fourth finger on string three for the 7th fret and on string two for the 8th fret.

Position 3 G Major/E Minor Pentatonic Pattern

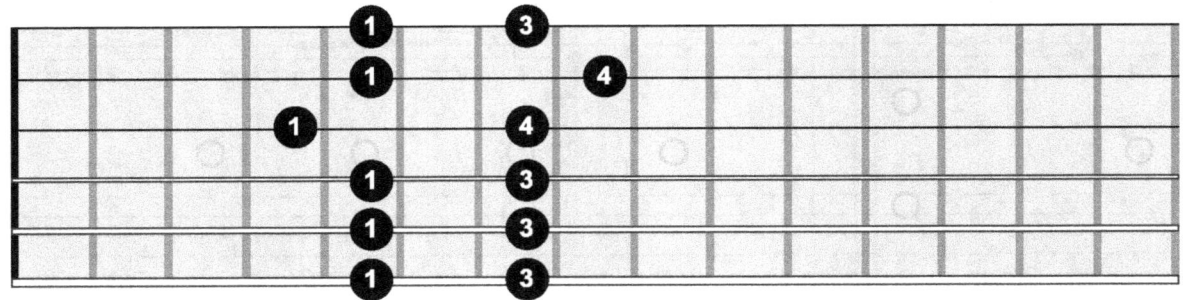

Warm-Up #32

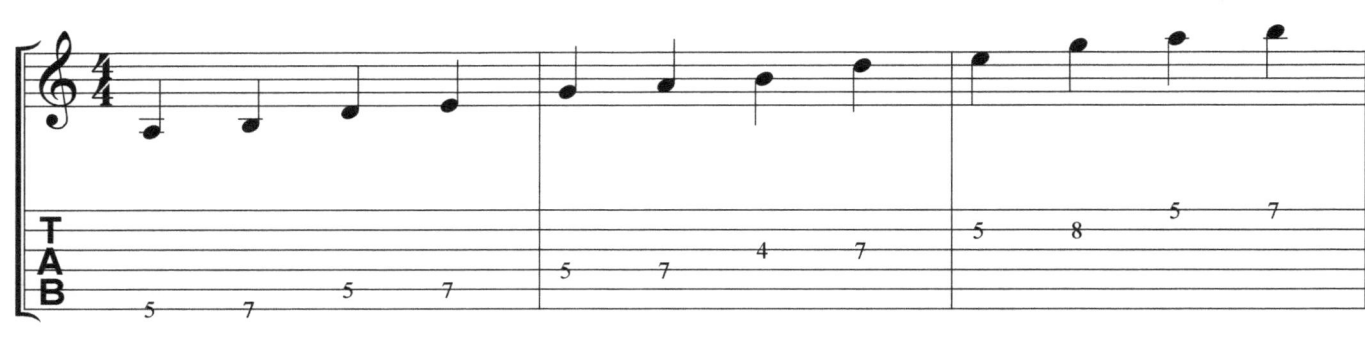

Warm-Up #33

Warm-Up #34

Warm-Up #35, #36, and #37

Warm-ups #35, #36, and #37 are all variations on the three notes up, one note back pattern.

Warm-Up #35

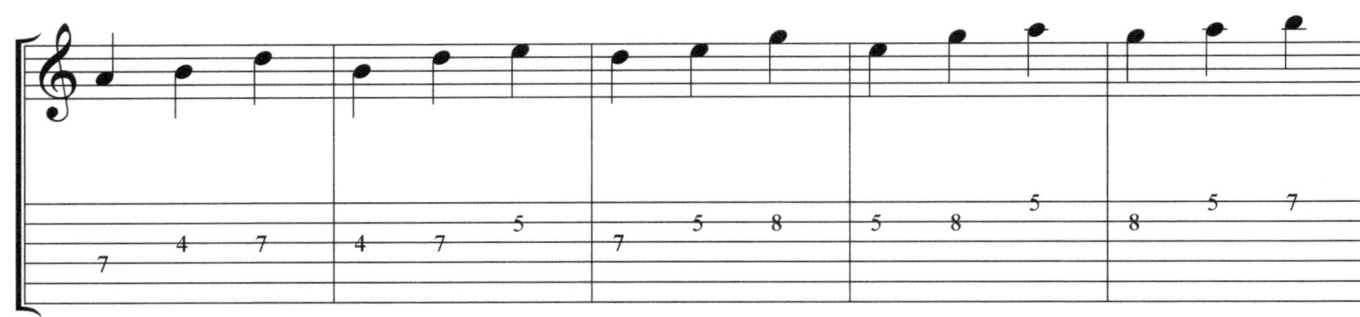
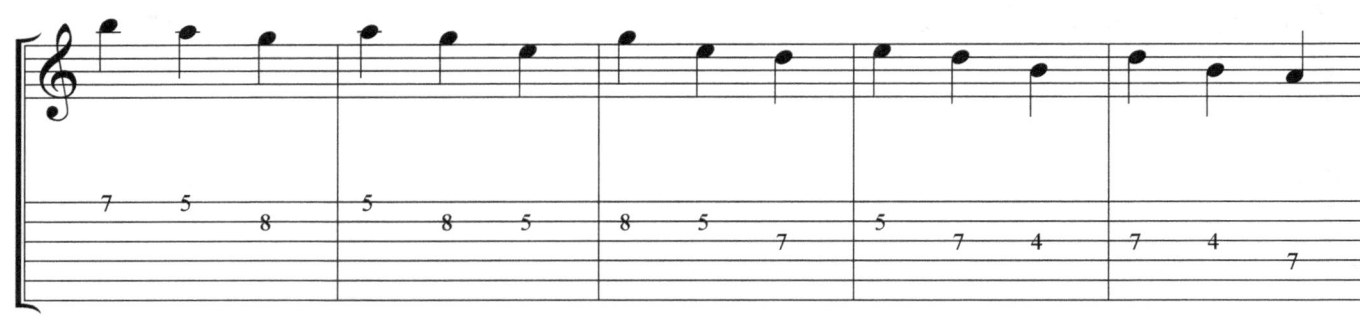
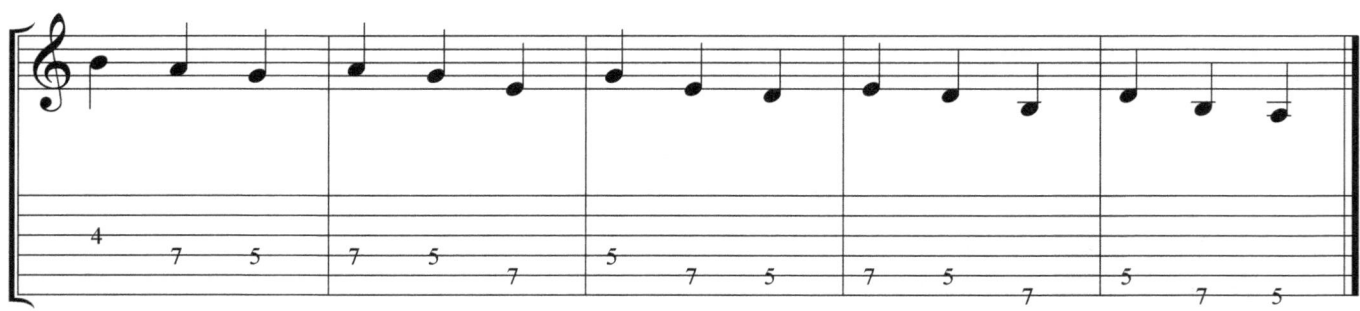

Warm-Up #36

Warm-Up #37

Warm-Up #38, #39, and #40

The following warm-ups skip a note while going through the entire pentatonic pattern in third position.

Warm-Up #38

Warm-Up #39

Warm-Up #40

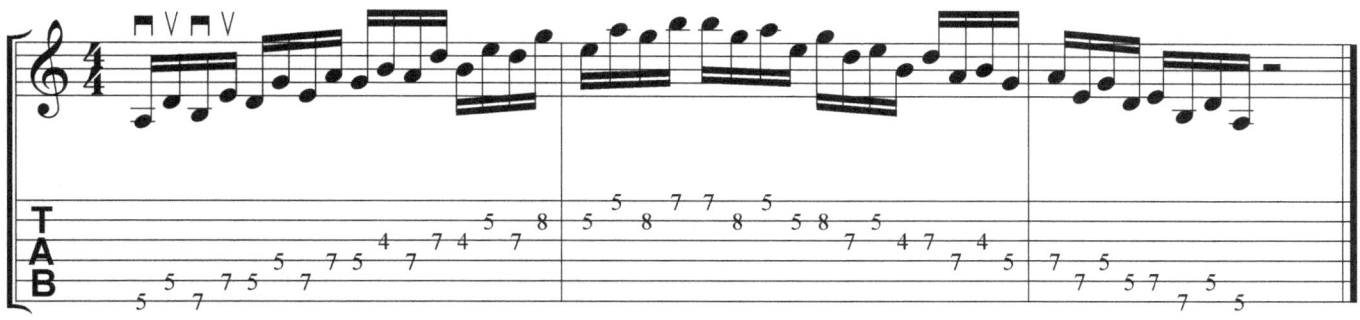

Warm-Ups #41 and #42

The next two warm-ups contain hammer-ons and pull-offs and are to be practiced just like their previous counterparts.

Warm-Up #41

Warm-Up #42

Warm-Up #43

This warm-up is a combination of positions 1, 2, and 3. Be sure to practice it in the same manner as all the other warm-ups: with a metronome, good technique, and gradually build speed.

The next three warm-ups are licks that cover all three positions.

Warm-Up #44

Warm-Up #45

Warm-Up #46

Unit 4: Position 4
G Major/E Minor Pentatonic Scale

Like Unit 3, Unit 4 contains a pattern of notes that does not start on either root. Therefore, warm-up #47 gives you a chance to practice the E minor pentatonic on the higher strings, and #48 simply drops that same scale one octave. So in this section there is no G major pentatonic presented in one octave.

Warm-Up #47

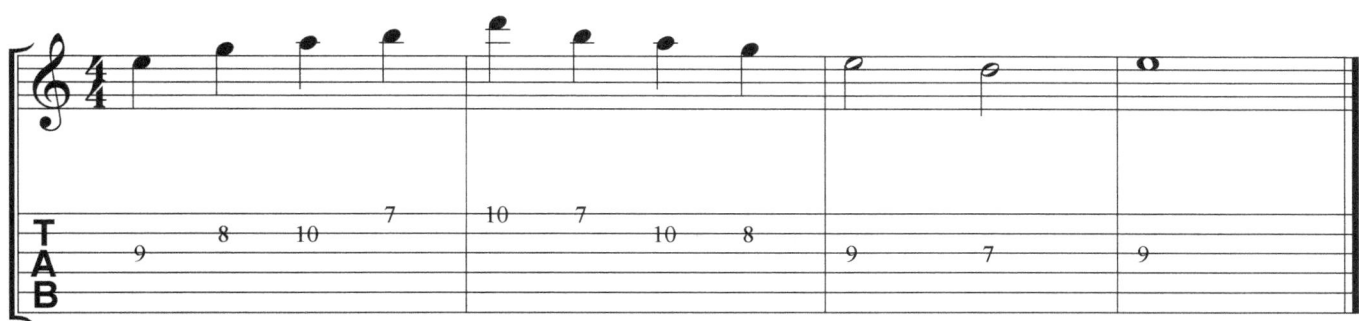

Warm-Up #48

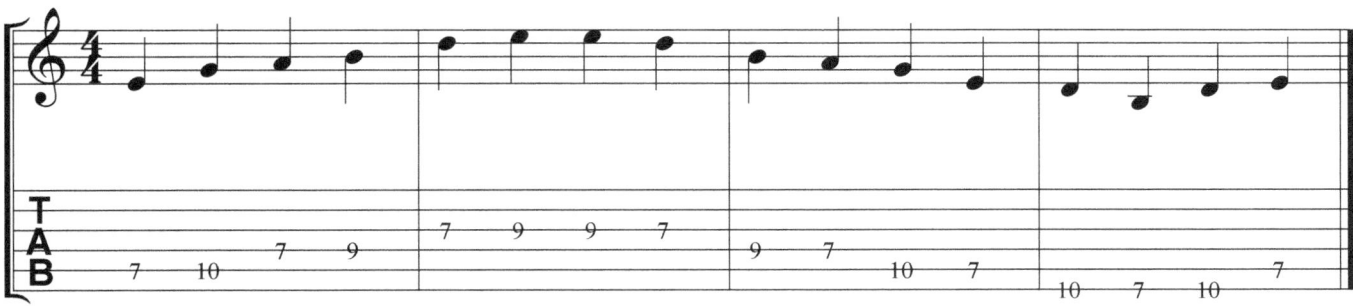

Warm-Ups #49, #50, and #51

The next three warm-ups present the full box pattern in this position using quarter notes, then eighth notes, then sixteenth notes. Be sure to continue to watch your technique and use a metronome.

Position 4 fingering

To start:

- Use your first finger for the note B on the 6th string, seventh fret. Then use your fourth finger (pinky) for the note D on the 6th string, tenth fret.

In general:

- Use your first finger for any note played on the seventh fret.
- Use your second finger for any note played on the eighth fret.
- Use your third finger for any note played on the ninth fret.
- Use your fourth finger for any note played on the tenth fret.

Position 4 G Major/E Minor Pentatonic Pattern

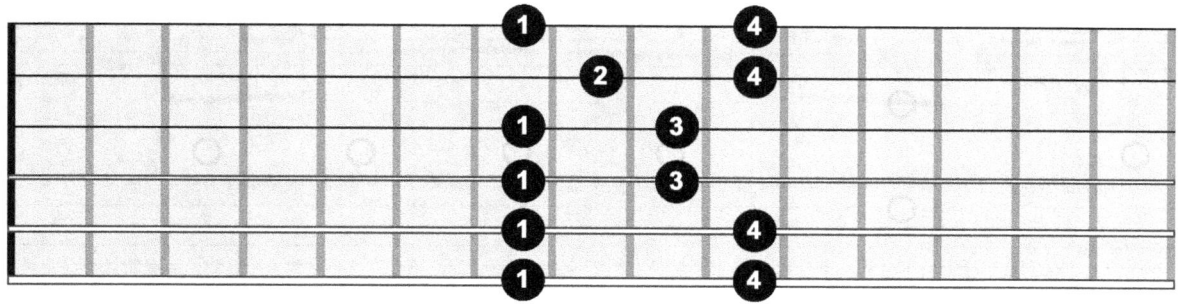

Warm-Up #49

Warm-Up #50

Warm-Up #51

Warm-Ups #52, #53, and #54

The next three warm-ups move up three notes of the scale and then back one.

Warm-Up #52

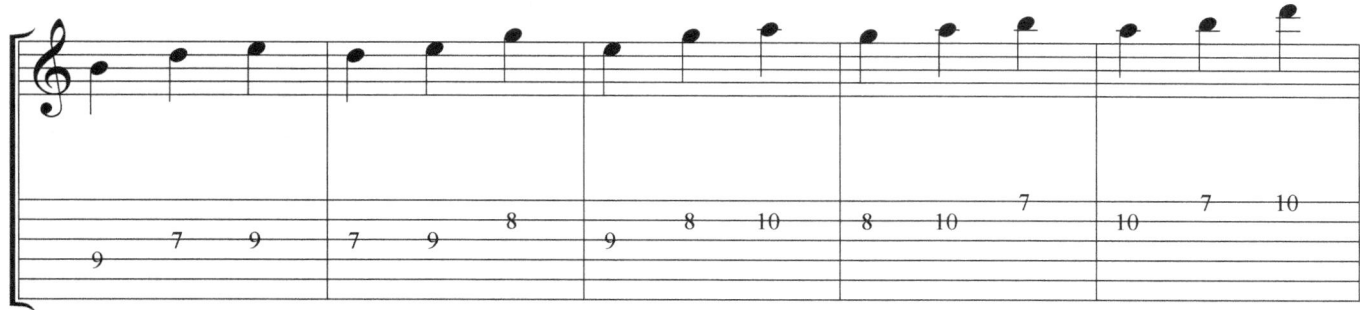
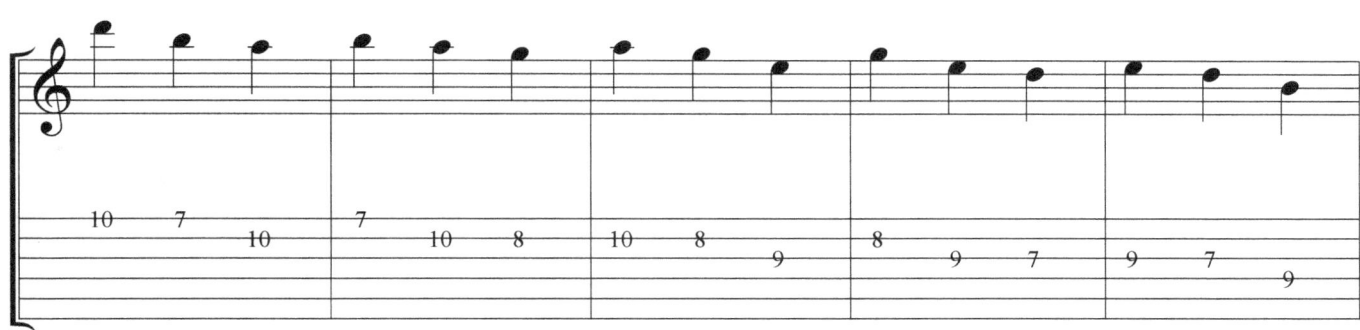

Warm-Up #53

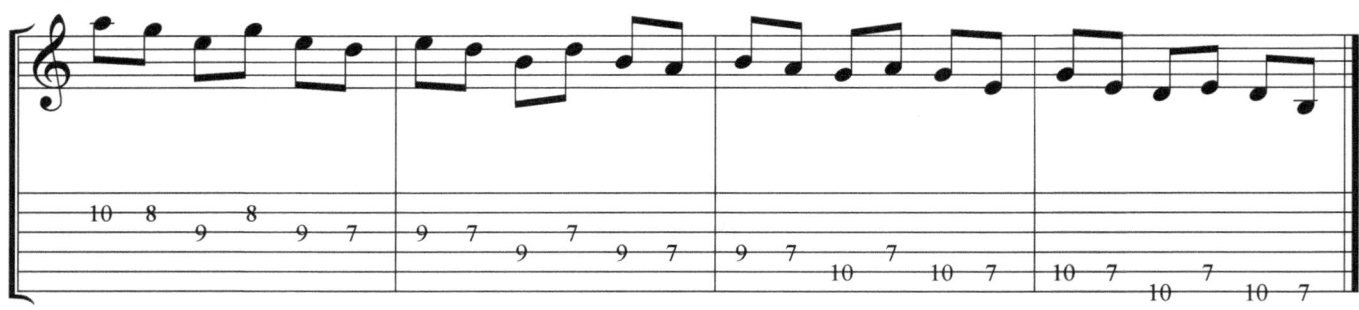

Warm-Up #54

Warm-Ups #55, #56, and #57

The following warm-ups move through the pentatonic pattern skipping a note.

Warm-Up #55

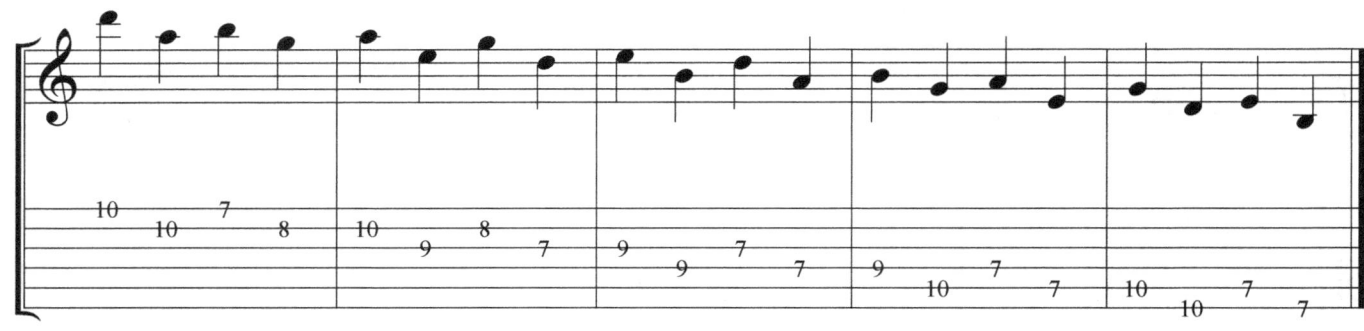

Warm-Up #56

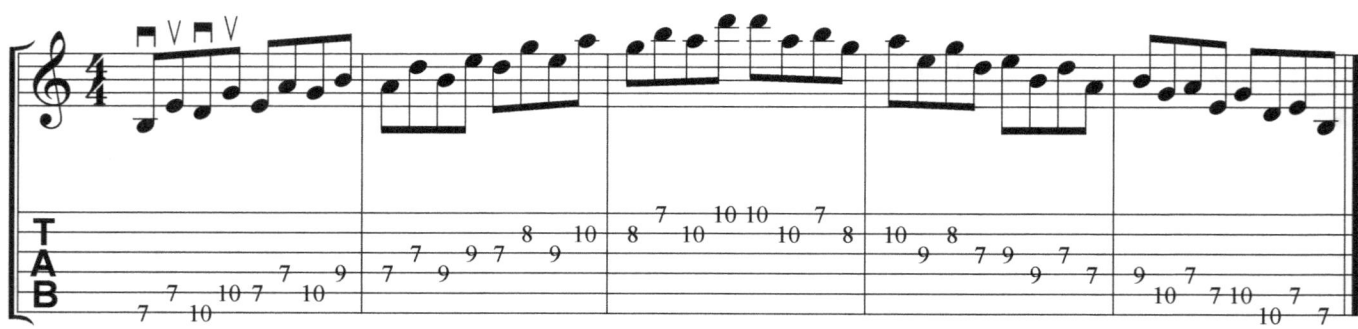

Warm-Up #57

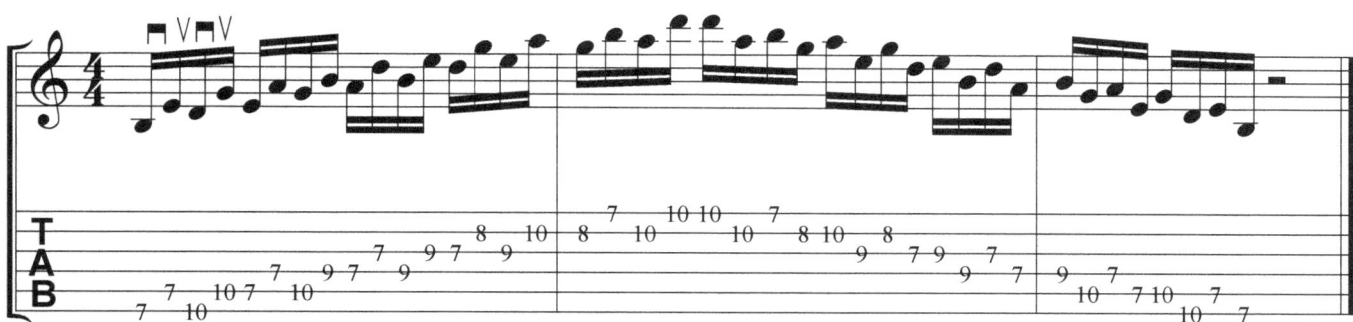

Warm-Up #58

Note that the next exercise contains hammer-ons and pull-offs. Reminder: watch your technique and always use a metronome.

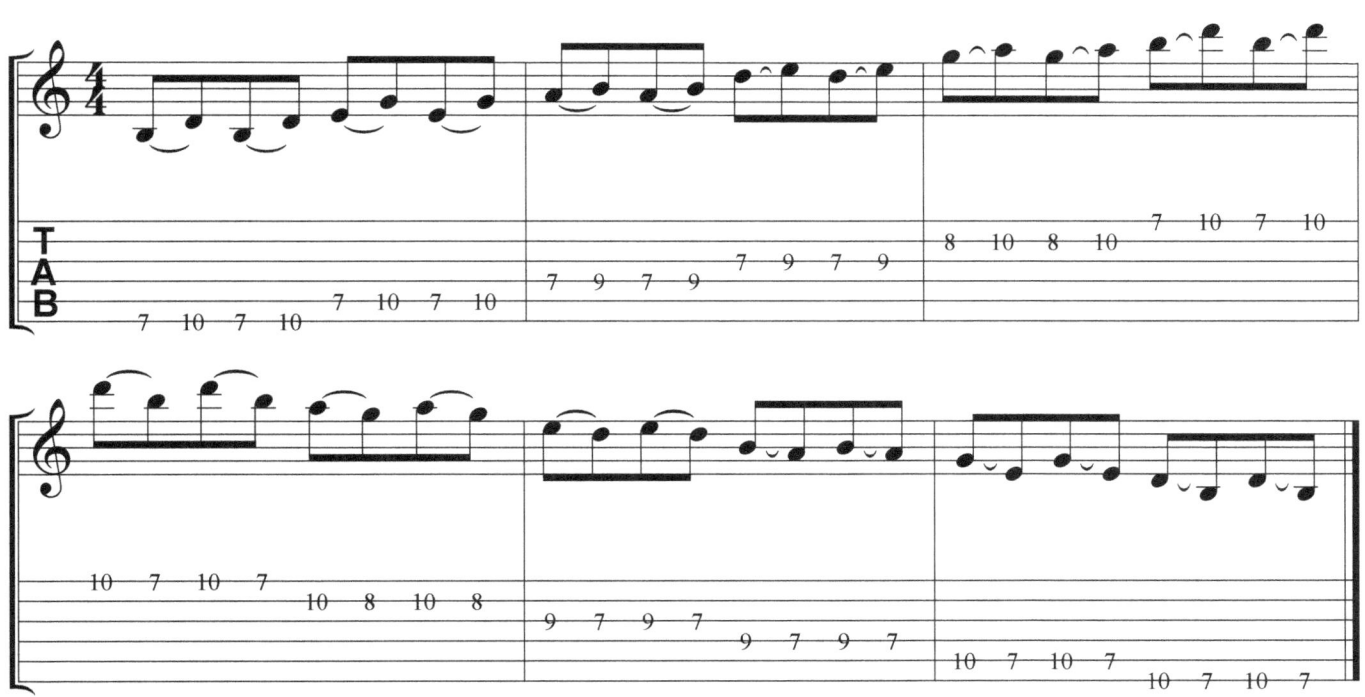

Warm-Up #59

The next warm-up combines all four positions into one exercise.

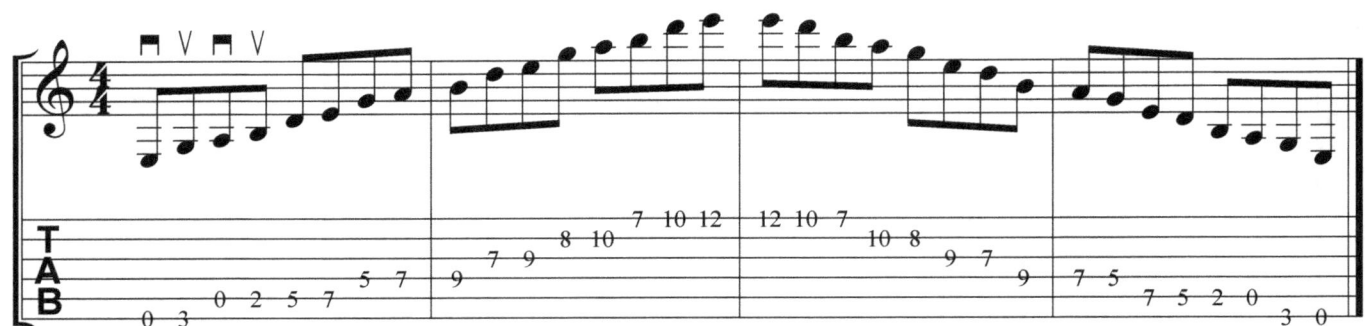

Warm-Ups #60, #61, and #62

Practice the following licks with a metronome. Like always, start slowly and gradually build speed.

Warm-Up #60

Warm-Up #61

Warm-Up #62

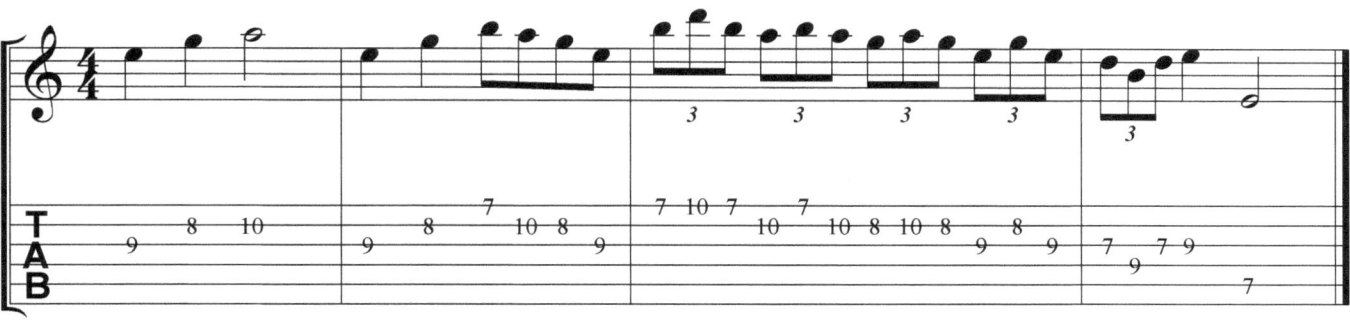

Unit 5: Position 5
G Major/E Minor Pentatonic Scale

Position 5 covers frets 9 through 12 and essentially completes the five pentatonic box patterns. Like the previous two positions, position 5 does not start on either of the two roots. As a result, the first two warm-ups in this unit divide the pattern into two one octave scales in E minor pentatonic.

Warm-Up #63

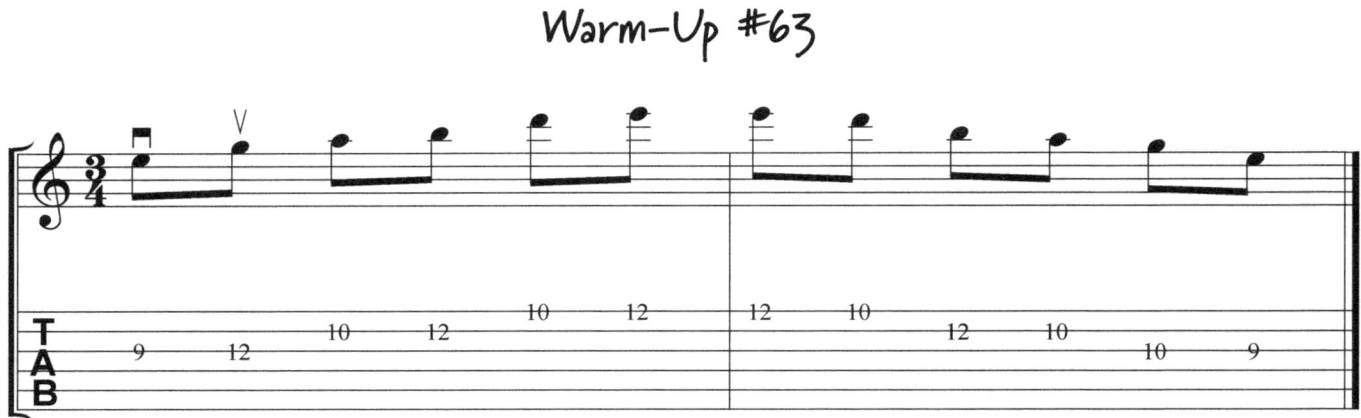

Warm-Up #64

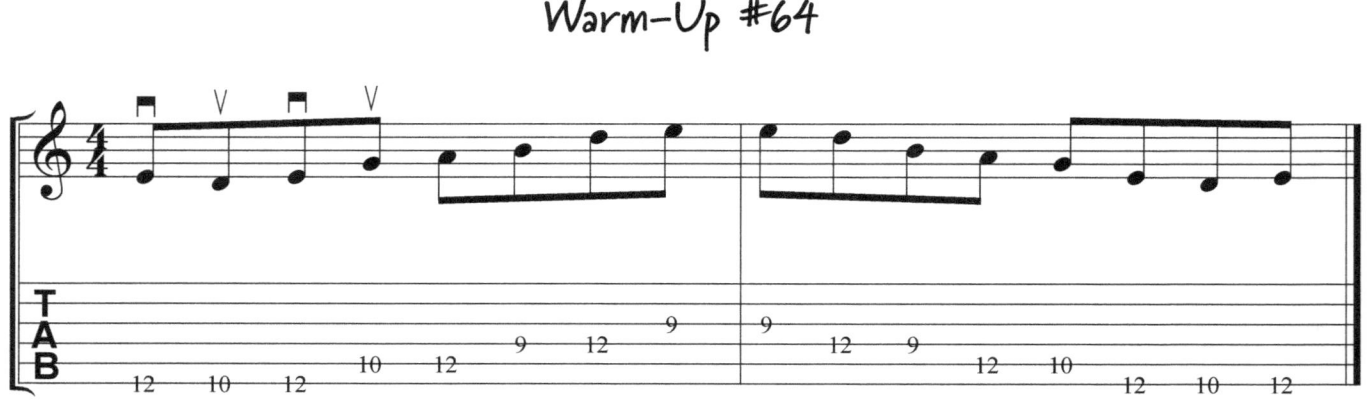

Warm-Ups #65, #66, and #67

The following three warm-ups contain the full box pattern for position 5.

Position 5 fingering

To start:

- Use your second finger for the note D on the 6th string, tenth fret. Then use your fourth finger (pinky) for the note E on the 6th string, twelfth fret.

In general:

- Use your first finger for any note played on the ninth fret.
- Use your second finger for any note played on the tenth fret.
- Use your fourth finger for any note played on the twelfth fret.

Position 5 G Major/E Minor Pentatonic Pattern

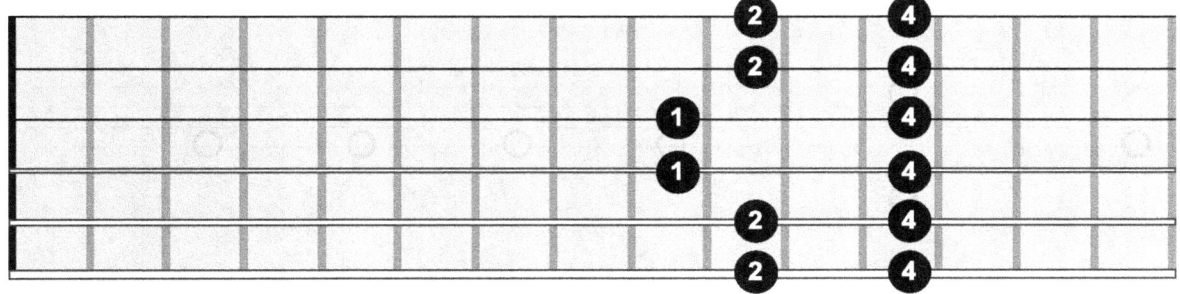

Warm-Up #65

Warm-Up #66

Warm-Up #67

Warm-Ups #68, #69, and #70

The warm-ups on the following pages move through the full box pattern going up three notes, then back one.

Warm-Up #68

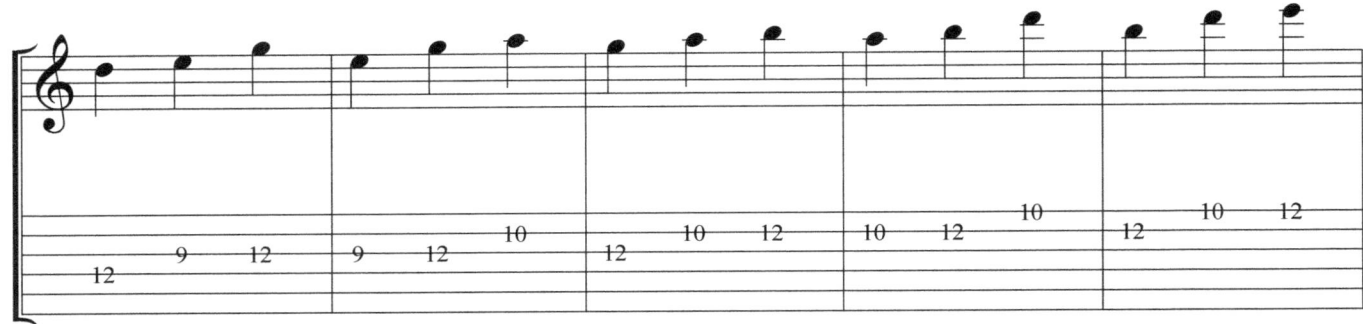
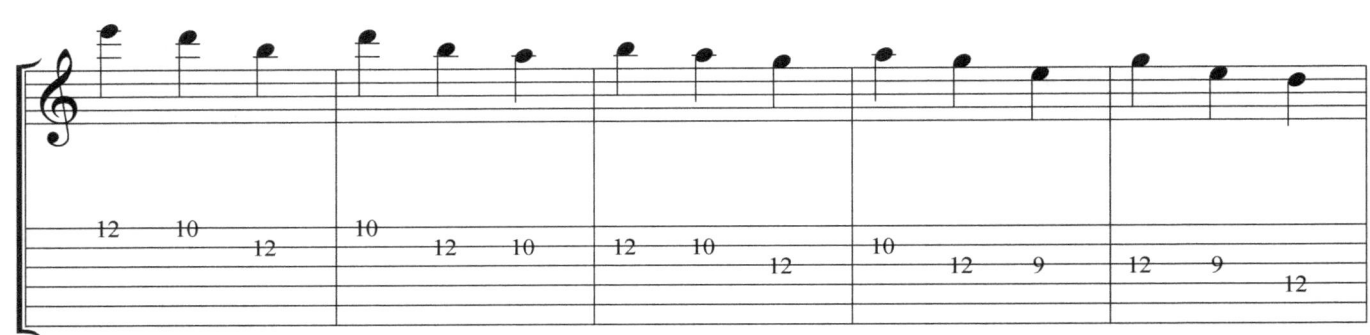

Warm-Up #69

Warm-Up #70

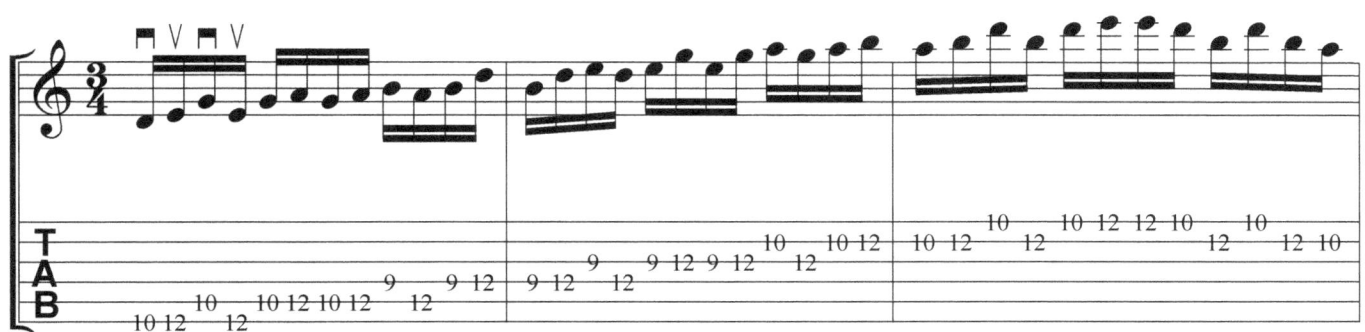
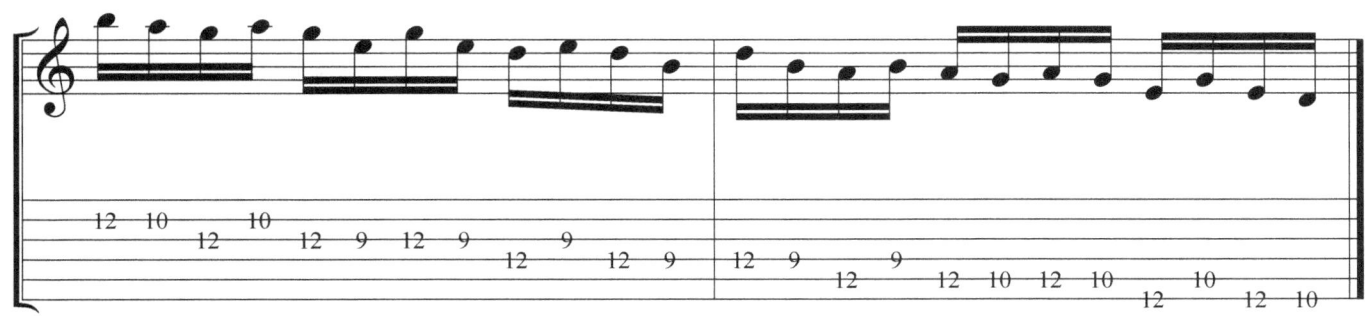

Warm-Ups #71, #72, #73

The next three warm-ups once again skip a note while moving through the pentatonic scale pattern.

Warm-Up #71

Warm-Up #72

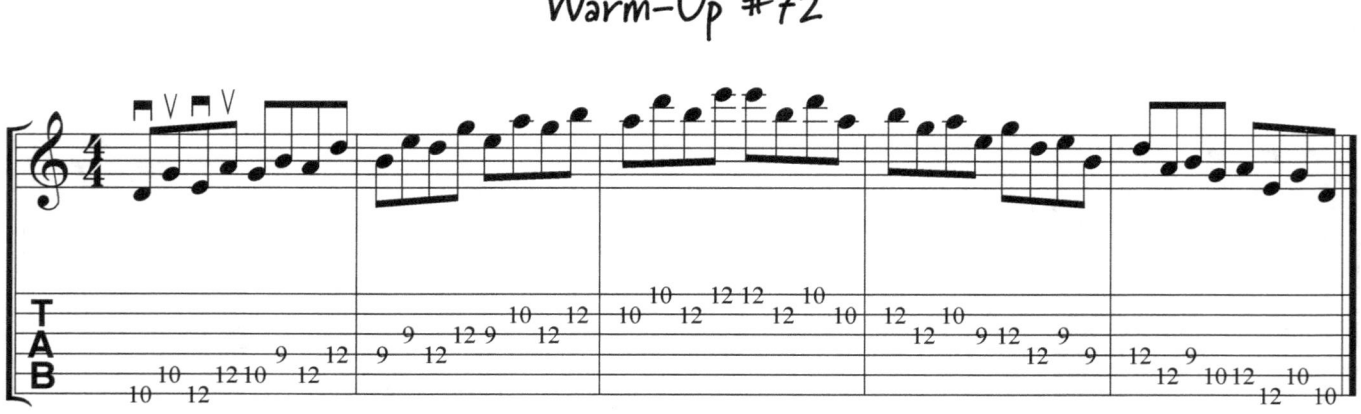

Warm-Up #73

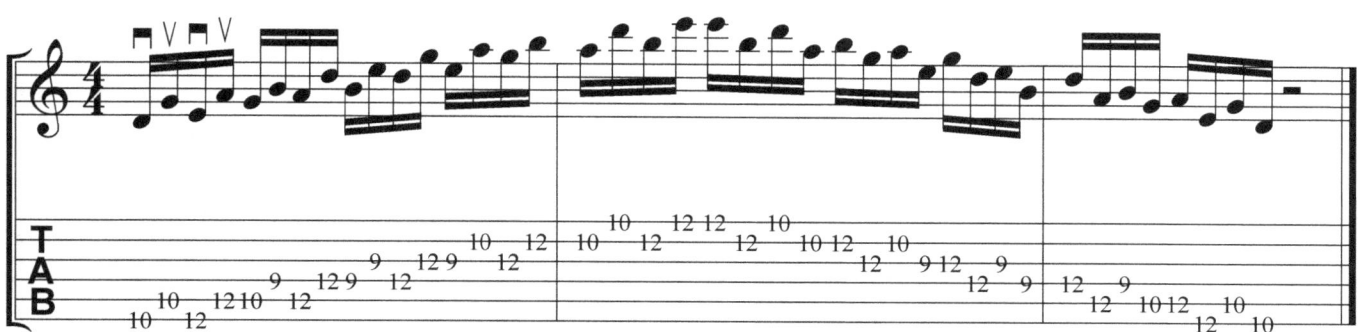

Warm-Up #74

Practice the Position 5 Pentatonic pattern with hammer-ons and pull-offs.

Warm-Up #75

The next warm-up combines patterns 4 and 5 together.

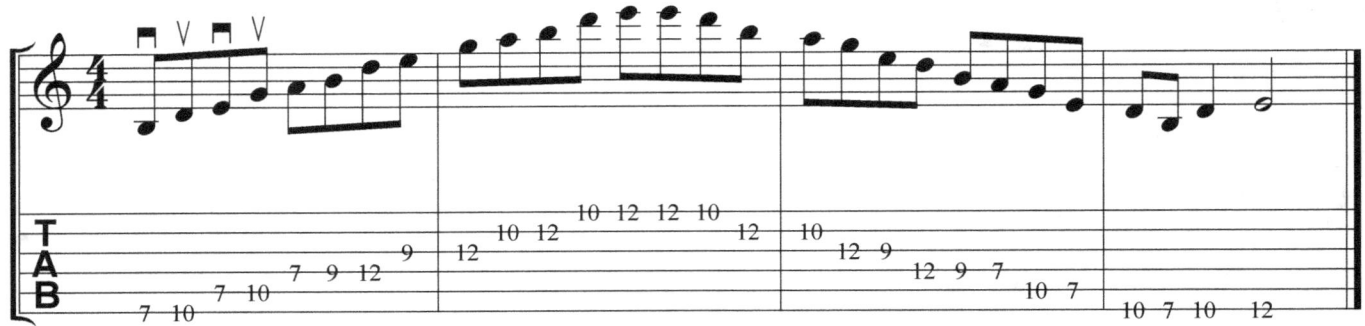

Warm-Up #76

Warm-up #76 combines all five patterns into one exercise.

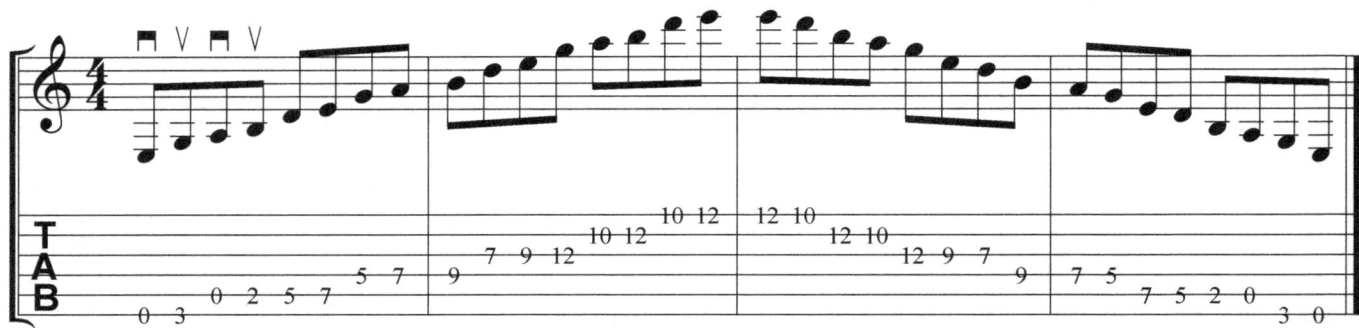

Warm-Ups #77, #78, and #79

The following licks are based on the Position 5 pattern.

Warm-Up #77

Warm-Up #78

Warm-Up #79

Unit 6: Position 6
G Major/E Minor Pentatonic Scale

Position 6 is the most widely used pentatonic pattern. It is also the pattern presented in Unit 1, but a full octave higher, so if it seems familiar, that's why. So just like all the other patterns, you'll want to use a metronome, play each slowly to start and then gradually build speed.

Warm-Up #80

Warm-Up #81

Warm-Up #82, #83, and #84

The next three warm-ups are based on the full box pattern.

Position 6 fingering

To start:

- Use your first finger for the note E on the 6th string, twelfth fret.
- Use your fourth finger for the note G on the 6th string, fifteenth fret.

In general:

- Use your first finger for any note played on the twelfth fret.
- Use your third finger for any note played on the fourteenth fret.
- Use your fourth finger for any note played on the fifteenth fret.

Position 6 G Major/E Minor Pentatonic Pattern

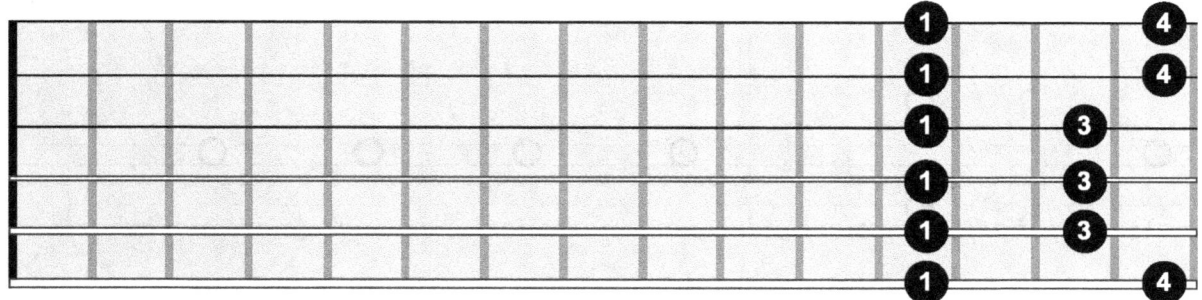

Warm-Up #82

Warm-Up #83

Warm-Up #84

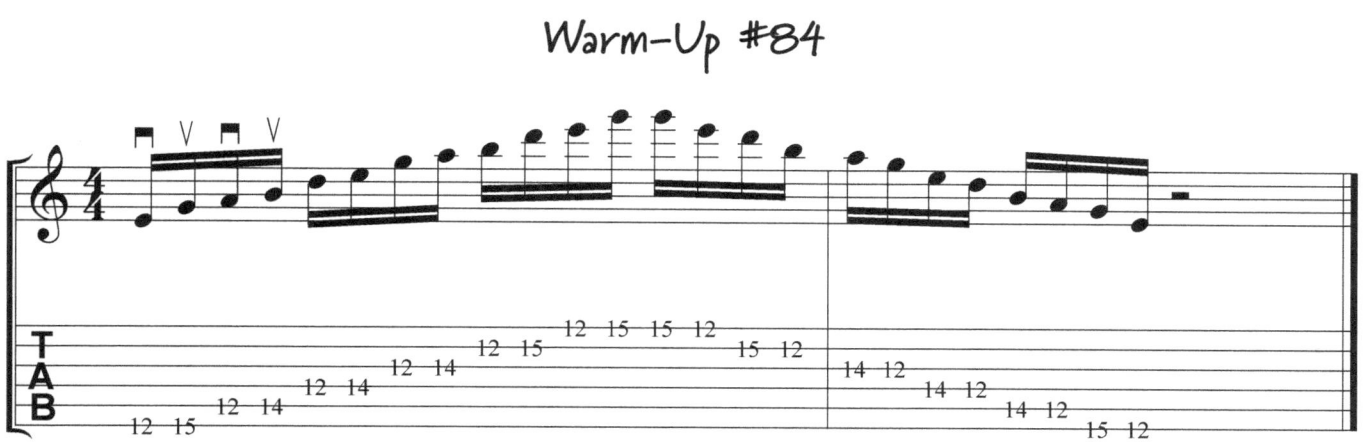

Warm-Up #85, #86, and #87

The next set of warm-ups move up three notes and then back one.

Warm-Up #85

68

Warm-Up #86

Warm-Up #87

Warm-Ups #88, #89, and #90

Warm-ups #88, #89, and #90 skip a note as they progress through the pentatonic pattern.

Warm-Up #88

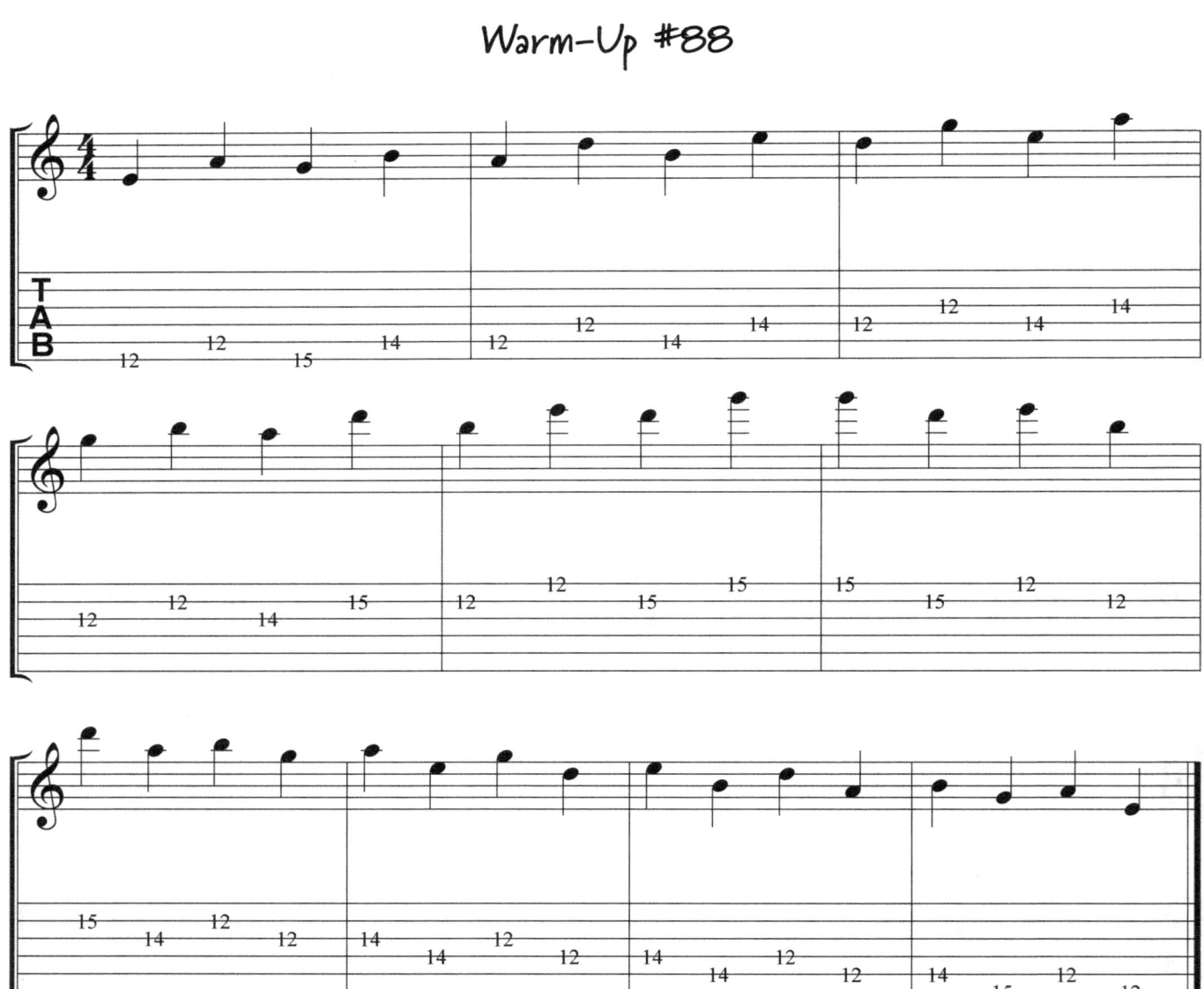

Warm-Up #89

Warm-Up #90

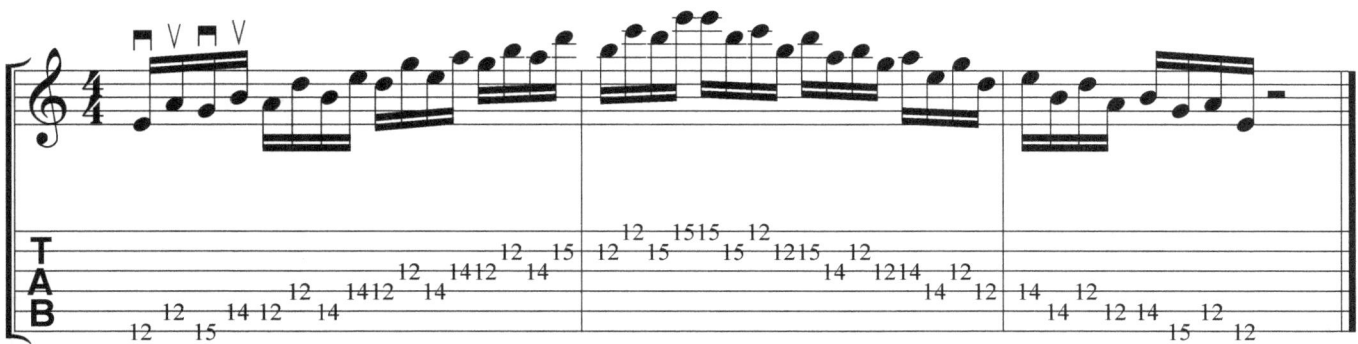

Warm-Up #91

The next warm-up includes hammer-ons and pull-offs.

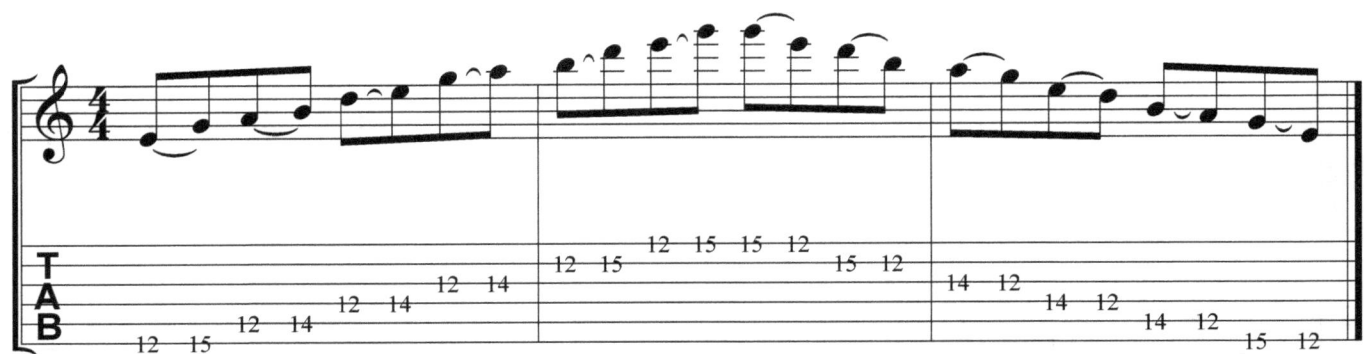

Warm-Ups #92 and #93

The next two warm-ups combine positions.

Warm-Up #92

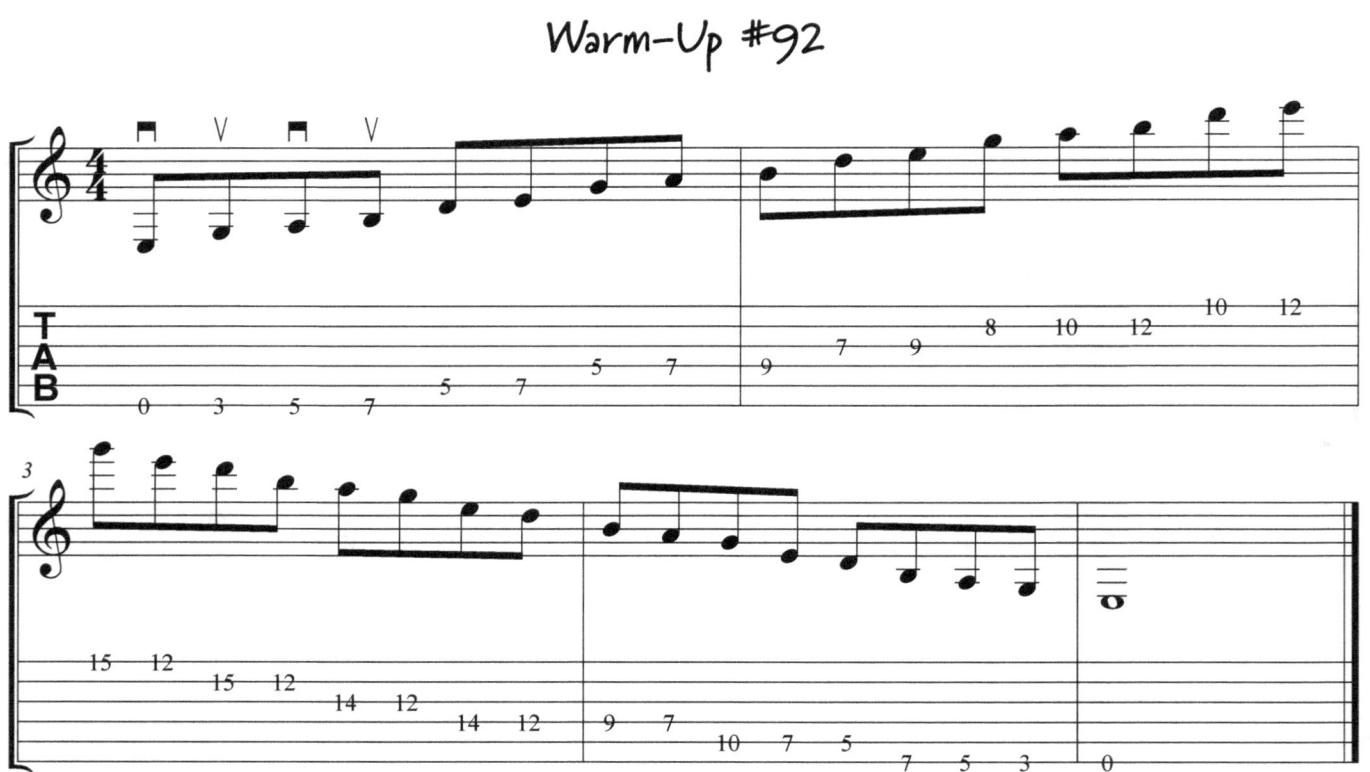

Warm-Up #93

Warm-Ups #94, #95, #96, and #97

The final four warm-ups are licks. The first three licks give you practice in position 6, whereas warm-up #97 covers the entire neck.

Warm-Up #94

Warm-Up #95

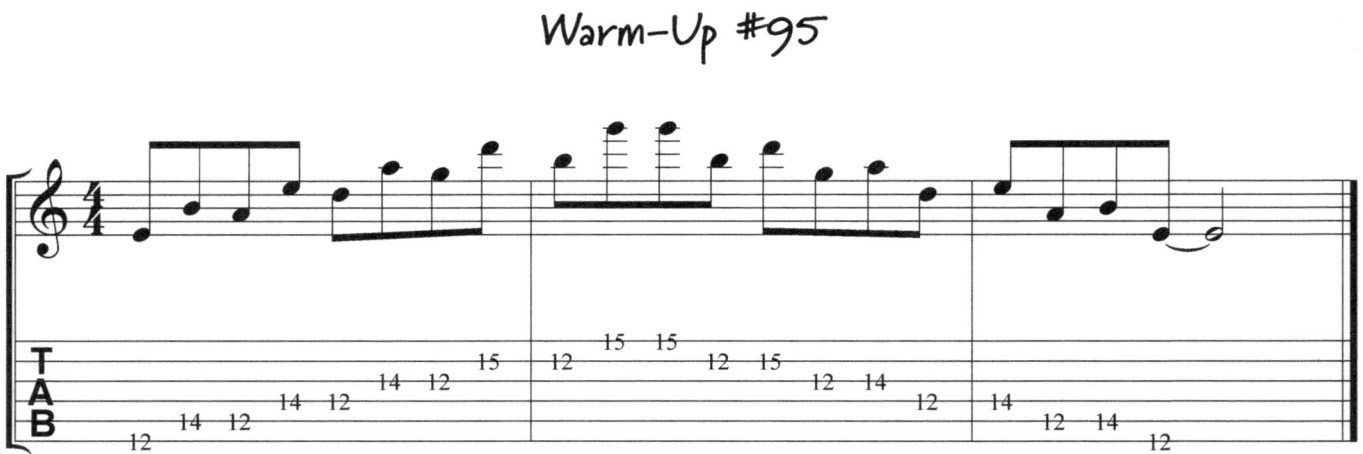

Warm-Up #96

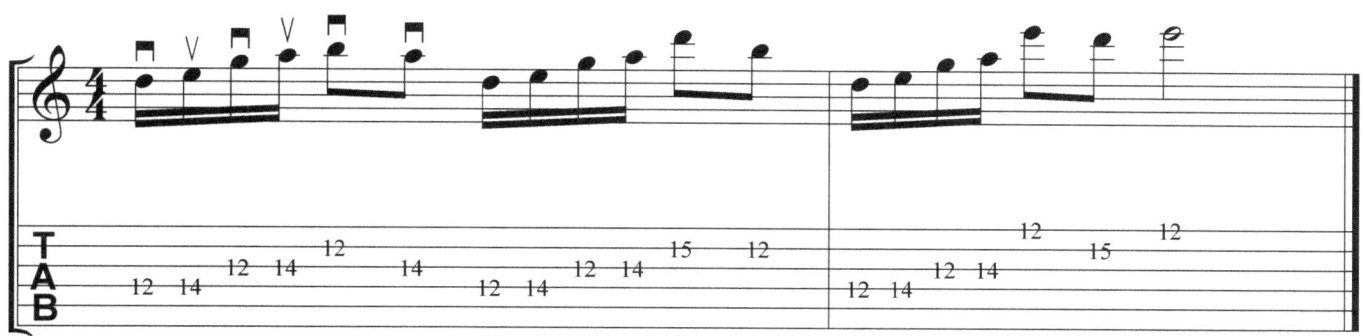

Warm-Up #97

Appendix

- How to Tune Your Guitar
- Introduction to Tablature
- Introduction to Reading Guitar Music
- How to Use a Metronome
- Pentatonic Positions Reference Chart

How to Tune Your Guitar

 The first thing you need to know in order to tune the guitar is what notes to tune to. The chart below shows the pitches of each string. Of course, if you are playing left-handed, these are reversed.

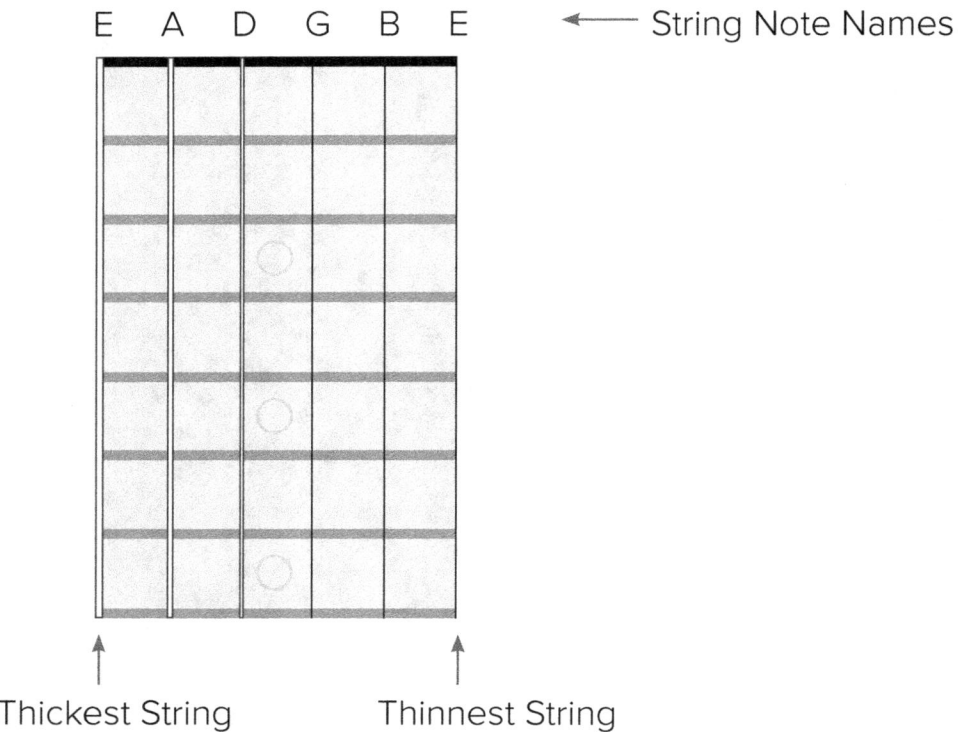

There are a couple of sayings that can help you remember the names of the strings, from thick to thin:

Eddie **A**te **D**ynamite, **G**ood **B**ye **E**ddie.

Or the less violent:

Every **A**mateur **D**oes **G**et **B**etter **E**ventually.

2 The second thing you should know is that tuning takes practice. It can be a little frustrating at first, but once you've done it a few times it gets easier and easier.

3 The third thing you need to know is that most of the time your guitar will only need slight adjustments. Once it's in tune, it will usually stay fairly close to in tune most of the time. However, it is recommended that you check your tuning every time you pick up the guitar. Be sure to listen carefully to the sound of an in-tune guitar so you become familiar with what it should sound like.

4 Now that you know this, we can begin tuning the guitar. There are several tuning methods. The best method is to buy a guitar tuner and learn how to use it. (You can find information on tuners on the next page.)

Typically, most tuners will show which note you are playing and then tell you whether or not the note is too low, too high, or in tune. Usually, a meter of some kind will display this information.

If the string is too low, you'll want to tighten the string, If the string is too high, you'll want to loosen it. Be sure to listen to the sound of the string as well. Your ear will help you figure out if you are going too far from the in-tune note.

Guitar Tuners and Other Tuning Resources

Tuners come in all shapes and sizes. There are credit card sized tuners, apps, and clip-on tuners that attach to your guitar. The best apps I've found for tuning include Pitchlab and GuitarTuna. However, there are many others that can work well and most of them are free.

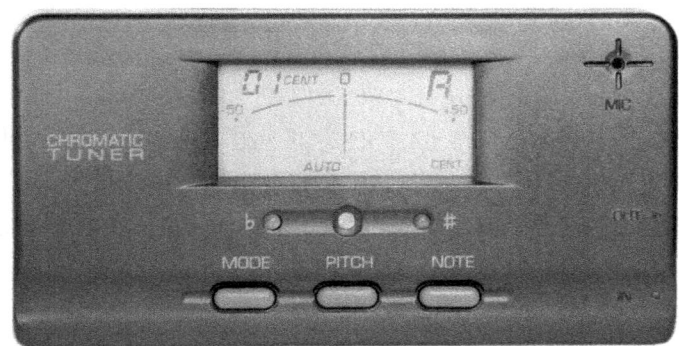

Another way you can tune the guitar is to use a reference pitch from an instrument that is already in tune. Most people use a piano, another in-tune guitar, or a pitch pipe to achieve this. In this case, you simply listen to the reference pitch and then match that pitch on your instrument. This can be difficult for beginners, but can help you to develop a strong ear as well as help you to develop your overall musicianship.

If you struggle with tuning, you might also try searching YouTube for lessons and suggestions on how to get your guitar in tune, as watching someone walk through the steps can be helpful as well.

How to Read Tablature

Tablature (or TAB) is the most popular way of learning new songs. It is almost as old as standard notation for stringed instruments. The advantages of TAB are that it's easy to read and allows you to figure out songs much faster than standard notation. However, there are some drawbacks. Most TABS do not include any rhythm, meaning you have to either know how the song is supposed to sound ahead of time or rely on the standard notation, when available.

Tablature shows you *where* to play, while standard notation shows you *what* to play. Therefore, both are equally as valuable when learning a new song.

To read tablature, each line represents a string on the guitar. The lowest string is the bottom line, and the highest string is the top line. (See below). Numbers are placed on the lines to show you which fret or frets to place your fingers. For example, if you see a number 1 on the first string (the top line), simply play the first fret on the first string. A zero tells you to play the open string.

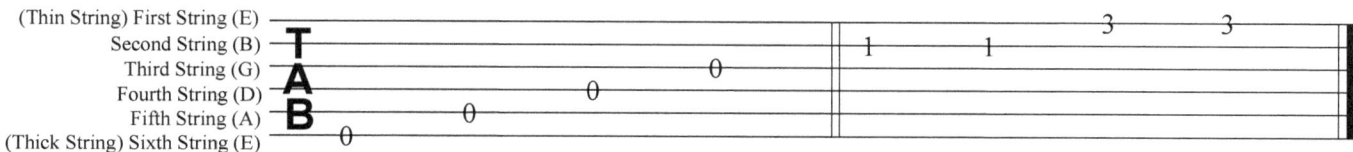

When reading tablature, the numbers on the lines represent the fret numbers.

The Elements of Reading Music

The Staff

Long ago there was no universal system to keep track of what a song sounded like. For a very long time, the only way to have a record of a song or piece of music was to pass it on from musician to musician by ear. Eventually, someone decided to place a circle on a line and call it a specific pitch. After some time, more lines were included, and the modern staff was born. The **staff** is simply a chart showing the highness and lowness of pitches. The lower a dot (or notehead) is on the staff, the lower the sound and vice versa.

In order to know which range of pitches to perform, clefs were used. A **clef** is a symbol that tells what notes to expect on the staff. There are several clefs in music, but for guitar we only need to learn one: the **treble clef**. (Though it is recommended to learn bass clef as well in order to develop your overall musicianship.)

Staff with Treble Clef

The treble clef tells you what specific notes, or pitches, you can expect to find on its lines and spaces. The lines are (from low to high) E G B D F. The spaces are F A C E. Many elementary schools teach a mnemonic device to help you remember these note names: Every Good Boy Does Fine. And of course the spaces spell FACE.

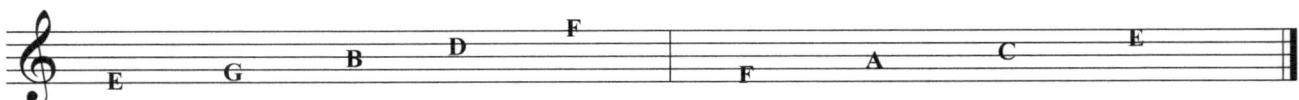

Ledger Lines

It is possible to go higher and lower than what is on the clef. When this is done, the extra notes are placed on lines called **ledger lines.**

In music there are a total of 12 notes that can occur at different pitch levels. Each different sound is given a letter name. Thus the musical alphabet consists of A B C D E F G. However, this represents only seven of these notes; the remaining five notes fall in between these and are designated either sharp or flat .

Understanding Time

The staff is divided up into sections called bars or measures. This is done to make the music easier to read and to help you figure out when to play the notes.

Each measure is only allowed a certain number of notes. This limitation allows us to keep track of time. The grouping of these notes is called meter. The most common meter is four beats per measure, or 4/4 time.

Beat is the underlying current of the music. You don't necessarily hear the beat. Think of it as a second hand on a clock, a constant steady clicking that helps you keep track of time.

What you actually play is rhythm. Rhythm tells you how long or how short a pitch should be held. For example, in 4/4 time a whole note is sustained for four beats. A half note is sustained for two beats. A quarter note (which takes up a quarter of a measure) is sustained for only one beat.

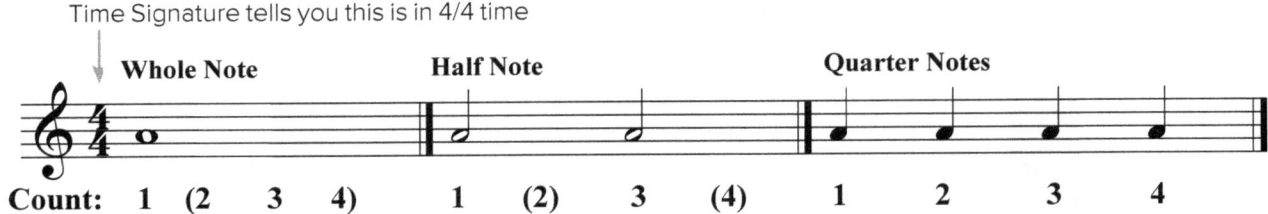

Besides 4/4 time, the second most common meter is 3/4. This means that there are only three beats per measure, instead of four, and the quarter note still represents the beat.

Eighth Notes

A quarter note can be further broken down into two eighth notes, each representing half a beat. When performing eighth notes, pick down on the downbeat, and up on the second half of each eighth note pair.

Eighth Notes

Sixteenth Notes

Eighth notes can be further broken down into four equal parts called sixteenth notes. That means that you can now play four notes for each beat. Just like eighth notes, sixteenth notes are often played using alternate picking. When counting sixteenth notes they are pronounced like this: One Eee And Uh, Two Eee and Uh, etc.

 If you'd like to learn more about note reading, check out The Missing Method for Guitar Note Reading Series. It'll take you through every note in every key!

Keeping Time: How to Use Your Metronome

When you are first starting any instrument, practicing with a metronome can seem frustrating or even impossible at times. The fact of the matter is that it is something you'll want to get good at and *can* once you know how. One obstacle that can get in the way is physical movement. For some, it won't yet be possible to move fast enough to lock in with the metronome; but don't worry, with practice and time you'll be able to use the metronome without any trouble.

There are many different types of metronomes out there, from the traditional wind-up, piano top metronome, to apps for your phone or tablet. They all work well and do about the same thing. Their purpose to provide the beat for you.

Step One: Synchronize with the Metronome

To start using the metronome, turn it on and select a relatively slow beat. I recommend somewhere around 50 beats per minute (bpm). Before you do anything, listen to the beat. Then begin by tapping your foot along with the beat. Be sure to anticipate each beat and play with the metronome. Don't wait for the click then tap your foot. Tap in sync with it.

Once you feel in sync with the metronome, begin to count out loud along with the clicks: 1, 2, 3, 4, over and over again. Keep your foot tapping while you do this. Feel the pulse; feel your footfalls; feel the time, and lock in.

Stop the metronome, but keep tapping at the same rate of speed. After about 30 seconds, turn the metronome back on to see how close you've come. Chances are you will have either sped up or slowed down. That's normal. Everyone has a different heart rate, and this can affect your perception of time. But with practice, you'll start to feel different tempos and different meters.

Step Two: Practice with the Metronome

Once you feel comfortable with step one, pick up your guitar and take some time to get in sync with the metronome. To do this, choose any open string and play this string while you tap your foot, listen to the click, and count out loud.

Next, try it with any chord. Simply tap your foot with the metronome clicking while you strum.

After that, take any song or exercise and play only the first full phrase or measure; that way you can focus on the time more so than on the pitches. After one phrase or measure is complete, move on to the next one, repeating the process. Once you have a couple of phrases or measures down with the metronome, turn it off again and try playing just as accurately without it.

The key here is that you DON'T want to try and play an entire song with the metronome yet. Instead, use it to help you focus your practicing of small sections, so you can play them more accurately.

Keep in mind that even seasoned professionals still use metronomes to practice. It's the best way to help you focus on your timing, which is crucial for playing with others, as well as sounding your best overall. Time is often overlooked by new players since the early focus is on the right notes, chords, or just getting your fingers in the right spots, but once you have all that, you have to be aware of and practice your timing.

The 5 Positions of the Pentatonic Scale

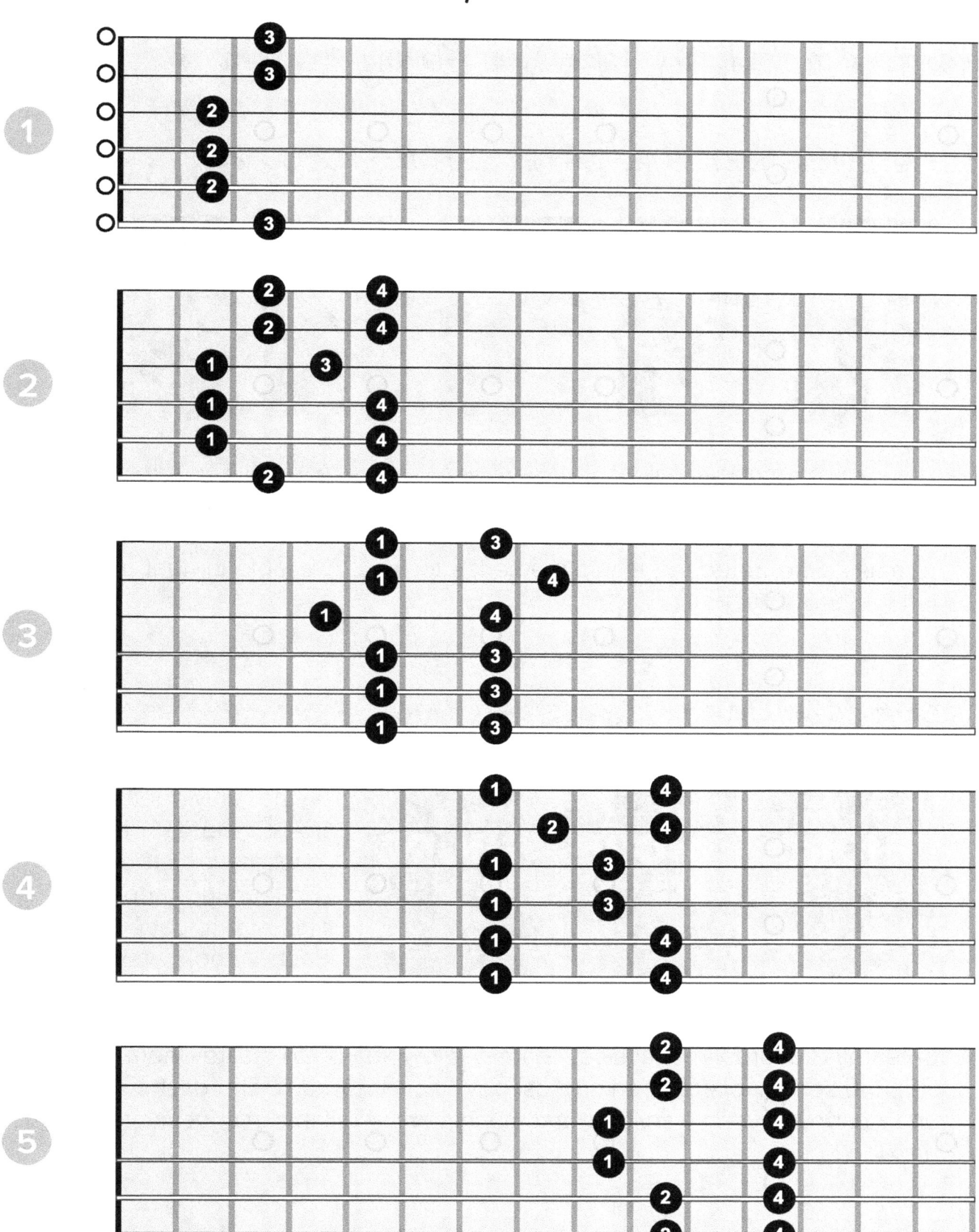

Resources to Help You Take Your Playing Further

The Missing Method for Guitar™ Note Reading Series

Unlock your musicianship with the power of note reading! The Missing Method for Guitar Note Reading series teaches you how to read every note on the guitar, from the open strings to the 22nd fret. If you are looking to master the fretboard, this is the series for you! Available in right and left-handed editions.

Guitar Chord Master™ Series

 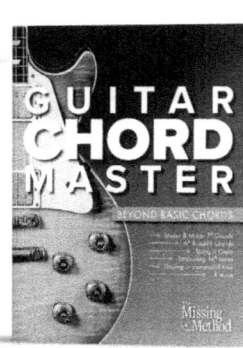 

Guitar Chord Master is the only method book series that focuses exclusively on learning chords and strum patterns. Each book takes you step-by-step through the process of learning chords in a musical context, allowing you to master them for life! The series covers open chords, power chords, barre chords, how to use a capo, moveable shapes, and much more. Available in right and left-handed editions.

Guitar Sheets™ Series

Blank TAB Paper, Chord Chart Paper, Staff Paper, Scale Chart Paper, Songwriting paper and more, bound in paperback to keep your best ideas handy! Need a bit of everything? Check out the first book in the series, the Guitar Sheets Collection, which includes TAB, Staff paper, TAB + Staff, Chord Chart Paper, and Scale Chart Paper. Each book includes useful bonus materials to help you improve.

Perfect Practice

Rethink how you practice. Stop practice burn-out. Learn the secrets to transforming your practice time into time well-spent. This book will help you to figure out how to identify and overcome the obstacles in your way by showing you what to practice and how to structure your time so you see results faster.

Find these and more at TheMissingMethod.com.

About the Author

Christian Triola is a professional guitar teacher and author with over 20 years experience using a scaffolding approach to instruction. This involves providing supports as students gain skills, then removing them as mastery develops. Christian has taught thousands of students in a way that enables them to learn and play music they love. He holds a Master's Degree in Education and a Bachelor's Degree in Music (Jazz Guitar) that help inform his student-centered approach. His books are designed to meet guitar learners' needs by filling gaps in existing methods. When he's not teaching, Christian enjoys writing fiction and hiking with his wife, Amy Joy.

What is the Missing Method?

We've helped thousands of students learn guitar through our step-by-step instructional materials. Our self-guided books for beginners explain guitar fundamentals in an easy-to-follow way. For building skills, we offer books on essential topics like note reading, scales, and chords, as well as a growing list of video courses and classes.

With our structured, skill-building approach, you'll become a better guitar player faster. Our materials provide ample practice so you can develop true mastery. Whether you're starting from scratch or looking to advance your skills, our books and courses will empower you to reach your guitar playing goals.

Learn more at TheMissingMethod.com.